Checklist of Library Building Design Considerations

Fifth Edition

William W. Sannwald

American Library Association
Chicago   2009

William W. Sannwald was assistant to the city manager and manager of library design and development from 1997 to 2004, and was city librarian of the San Diego Public Library from 1979 to 1997. He is now a full-time faculty member in the business school at San Diego State University and works as a library building and administrative consultant. He is the author of numerous books and articles on library architecture and management and has presented papers at national and international conferences. Past president of the Library Administration and Management Association (LAMA), Sannwald was a jury member of the joint ALA/AIA awards. He is the recipient of the San Diego AIA chapter's highest honor, the Irving Gill Award, for his contributions to library architecture.

While extensive effort has gone into ensuring the reliability of information appearing in this book, the publisher makes no warranty, express or implied, on the accuracy or reliability of the information, and does not assume and hereby disclaims any liability to any person for any loss or damage caused by errors or omissions in this publication.

The paper used in this publication meets the minimum requirements of American National Standard for Information Sciences—Permanence of Paper for Printed Library Materials, ANSI Z39.48-1992. ∞

Library of Congress Cataloging-in-Publication Data
Sannwald, William W.
    Checklist of library building design considerations / William W. Sannwald. —
  5th ed.
        p.   cm.
    Includes bibliographical references.
    ISBN 978-0-8389-0978-2 (alk. paper)
    1. Library architecture—United States. I. Title.
Z679.2.U54S36 2009
727'.8—dc22   2008030265

ISBN-13: 978-0-8389-0978-2

Printed in the United States of America

13 12 11 10 09   5 4 3 2 1

Contents

Preface   vii

1. **Building Planning and Architecture**

   A. Indicators of Dissatisfaction with Existing Facilities   1
   B. Institutional Planning Team   2
   C. Determining Space Needs   3
   D. Joint Use Considerations   6
   E. Alternatives to New Construction   8
   F. Selecting a Library Building Consultant   9
   G. Choosing an Architect   10
   H. Choosing a Contractor   14
   I. Architectural Design   15

2. **Library Site Selection**

   A. General Conditions   19
   B. Location   21
   C. Accessibility   22
   D. Size   23
   E. Environmental Issues   24

3. **Sustainable Design**

   A. Sustainable Sites   26
   B. Water Efficiency   29
   C. Energy and Atmosphere   30
   D. Materials   31
   E. Indoor Environmental Air Quality   32
   F. Lighting and Day Lighting   34
   G. Roofs   35

4. **General Exterior Considerations**

   A. Landscaping   36
   B. Parking   38
   C. Building Exterior   40
   D. Roof   41
   E. Bicycle Racks   42
   F. Flagpole   42
   G. Exterior Signage   43
   H. Loading Docks and Delivery   44
   I. Outdoor Trash Enclosures   47
   J. Outdoor Book and Media Returns   48

5. **Interior Organization of Library Buildings**

   A. Entrance   50
   B. Circulation Desk Facilities   53
   C. Reference Facilities   56
   D. Information Commons   60
   E. Multimedia Facilities   62
   F. Media Production and Presentation Labs   63
   G. Special Collections/Rare Books/Archives   64
   H. Reserve Book Room   67
   I. Faculty/Graduate Carrels and Study Rooms   68
   J. Literacy Center   68
   K. Young Adult Facilities   69
   L. Children's Facilities   71
   M. Meeting and Seminar Rooms   74
   N. Convenience Facilities   77
   O. Displays   80
   P. Public Art   81
   Q. Interior Signage   83
   R. Workrooms/Offices   85
   S. Staff Lounge   87
   T. Friends of the Library   88
   U. Library Store   90
   V. Interior Storage   92

6. Compliance with ADA Accessibility
    Guidelines

    A. Transportation, Parking Lots, Parking
        Signage, and Accessible Routes   93
    B. Ground and Floor Surfaces   95
    C. Curb Cuts   96
    D. Ramps   97
    E. Stairs   98
    F. Lifts and Elevators   99
    G. Doors   101
    H. Entrances   102
    I. Accessible Routes within the Building 104
    J. Drinking Fountains   105
    K. Water Closets   106
    L. Toilet Rooms   107
    M. Toilet Stalls   107
    N. Urinals   108
    O. Lavatories   109
    P. Handrails and Grab Bars   110
    Q. Controls and Operating Mechanisms   111
    R. Alarms   112
    S. Signage   113
    T. Telephones   115
    U. Fixed or Built-in Seating and Tables 116
    V. Assembly Areas   117
    W. Building Assistance Facilities   118

7. Telecommunications, Electrical,
    and Miscellaneous Equipment

    A. General Considerations   120
    B. Telecommunications Entrances
        and Closets   121
    C. Horizontal Pathways   122
    D. Cabling and Outlets   124
    E. Wireless Technology   125
    F. Workstation Connections   127
    G. Workstation Equipment   128
    H. Telephone System   128
    I. Miscellaneous Electrical Equipment   130
    J. Electrical Power   131

8. Interior Design and Finishes

    A. Service Desks   133
    B. Seating   135
    C. Tables   138
    D. Lighting   139
    E. Windows   140
    F. Flooring   141
    G. Walls   142
    H. Color   143
    I. Equipment List   144
    J. Behavioral Aspects of Space   150

9. Materials Handling and Storage:
    Book Stacks and Shelving

    A. Conventional Stationary Stacks
        and Shelving   155
    B. Movable-Aisle Compact Shelving   158
    C. Automated Storage and Retrieval
        System (ASRS)   160
    D. Materials Handling Systems   161
    E. Remote Storage   162

10. Building Systems

    A. Acoustics   165
    B. Heating, Ventilating, Air-Conditioning,
        and Refrigerating (HVAC&R) Systems   168
    C. Electrical Systems   170
    D. Lighting   172
    E. Plumbing and Restrooms   175
    F. Elevators and Escalators   177

11. Safety and Security

    A. General   178
    B. External Security   178
    C. Internal Security   179
    D. Fire Safety   181
    E. Disaster Planning   181

12. **Maintenance of Library Buildings and Property**

    A. Routine Maintenance   184
    B. Graffiti   186
    C. Building Materials   187
    D. Custodial Facilities   188
    E. Groundskeeper Facilities   189
    F. Trash Enclosures   189
    G. Betterments and Improvements   190

13. **Building Occupancy and Post-occupancy Evaluation**

    A. Building Acceptance   191
    B. Getting Ready for Occupancy   193
    C. Moving   194
    D. Post-occupancy Evaluation   195

14. **Groundbreaking and Dedication Ceremonies**

    A. Planning   198
    B. Event Checklist   200

Bibliography   205

Preface

This fifth edition of *Checklist of Library Building Design Considerations* is published to accomplish a number of goals:

- to assist librarians, architects, administrators, and other members of a building design team in programming library spaces

- to serve as a guide during the various stages of the design process in order to make sure that all needed spaces and functions are included in the library design

- to enable the evaluation of existing library spaces as part of a library's needs assessment process

- to provide data and support to the library in its presentations to governing authorities and stakeholder groups

The checklist includes questions concerning almost every aspect of space and function in a library building. The purpose of these questions is to make sure that the building design team in the evaluation and programming of spaces overlooks no element of the building. Although the list is probably not exhaustive, answering the questions in this document should ensure that no major design elements have been overlooked.

The checklist is a valuable tool for programming and planning existing and potential library buildings. Most of the basic areas listed apply to college and university, public, school, and special libraries. It should be relatively easy to adapt the checklist to meet the requirements of almost any type of library.

The first edition was adapted from a checklist produced by doctoral students in the School of Library and Information Studies at Texas Woman's University in Denton and was a product of the Library Building and Equipment Section's Architecture for Public Libraries Committee.

All sections in the fifth edition have been reviewed, revised, and updated. In addition some new chapters and sections are included:

- chapter 3, "Sustainable Design," a new chapter dealing with sutainable design, including site selection, water efficiency, energy and atmosphere, materials, and indoor environmental air quality

- in chapter 4, "General Exterior Considerations," new sections dealing with exterior conditions including loading docks and delivery, trash enclosures, and outdoor book and media returns

- in chapter 5, "Interior Organization of Library Buildings," new sections on information commons, media production and presentation labs, special collections, faculty/graduate carrels and study rooms, and public art

- chapter 6, "Compliance with ADA Accessibility Guidelines," reorganized to follow the same organizational scheme found in the federal law

- in chapter 7, "Telecommunications, Electrical, and Miscellaneous Equipment," a new section on wireless technology

- in chapter 8, "Interior Design and Finishes," a new section dealing with the behavioral aspects of space
- in chapter 9, "Materials Handling and Storage," a new section dealing with materials handling systems
- in chapter 11, "Safety and Security," a new section on disaster planning
- in chapter 12, "Maintenance of Library Buildings and Property," new sections on routine maintenance and betterments and improvements
- in chapter 13, "Building Occupancy and Post-occupancy Evaluation," a new section dealing with building acceptance

In 2004, I took early retirement from the City of San Diego, where I had served for twenty-four years as library director and assistant to the city manager. I was asked to teach full-time in the management department of the business school at San Diego State University, where I had taught part-time for over twenty years. I now teach upper-division undergraduate and MBA students in a variety of courses including organizational behavior, strategic management, internships, and ethics. It is a great experience, but I continue to stay involved in libraries through consulting, speaking, and writing.

I dedicate this fifth edition to my children: Sara A. Sannwald, William H. Sannwald, and Suzanne A. Sannwald. I am pleased and proud that my son, Bill, works in a library and is in library school; his wife, Suzanne, works with technology in a library-related job.

This publication should be viewed as a living document, and all comments and suggestions for future editions are welcome. Please send them to

William W. Sannwald
3538 Paseo Salamoner
La Mesa, CA 91941
Sannwald@mail.sdsu.edu

Building Planning and Architecture

	YES	NO	N/A

A. Indicators of Dissatisfaction with Existing Facilities

1. Has the mission of the library changed? ☐ ☐ ☐

   Comments: _____

2. Has the population served by the library increased or decreased? ☐ ☐ ☐

   Comments: _____

3. Have the demographics of the population served by the library changed? ☐ ☐ ☐

   Comments: _____

4. Has the library formed a partnership or alliance with another institution that requires a change in the physical building? ☐ ☐ ☐

   Comments: _____

5. Are there problems with the physical condition of the building (outdated systems, inflexible floor plans, Americans with Disabilities Act [ADA] problems, difficulty in installing technology)? ☐ ☐ ☐

   Comments: _____

6. Does the existing building hinder the delivery of good service? ☐ ☐ ☐

   Comments: _____

	YES	NO	N/A

7. Is there enough room for the products and services the library offers? ☐ ☐ ☐
    Comments: _____
    _____

8. In order to accommodate collection growth, have seats been exchanged for stacks? ☐ ☐ ☐
    Comments: _____
    _____

9. Is the atmosphere of the library pleasing to customers and staff? ☐ ☐ ☐
    Comments: _____
    _____

10. Has the mix of products and services offered by the library changed? ☐ ☐ ☐
    Comments: _____
    _____

B. Institutional Planning Team

1. Has an institutional library planning team been formed? ☐ ☐ ☐
    Comments: _____
    _____

2. Who are the members of the library planning team
    a) A representative of the legal owner (university, school, city, etc.) ☐ ☐ ☐
    b) Library representatives ☐ ☐ ☐
    c) Users (faculty, students, citizens, etc.) ☐ ☐ ☐
    d) Other representatives with technical skills such as engineering, legal, financial, architectural, building ☐ ☐ ☐
    e) Others (Friends of the Library, library committee members, etc.) ☐ ☐ ☐
    Comments: _____
    _____

3. What roles will members of the library planning team play
    a) Advising (gathering and disseminating information about the project) ☐ ☐ ☐
    b) Innovating (suggesting new ideas or new ways of tackling old problems) ☐ ☐ ☐
    c) Promoting ("selling" the project to interested stakeholders) ☐ ☐ ☐
    d) Developing (assessing and developing ideas for practical implementation) ☐ ☐ ☐
    e) Maintaining (ensuring that the infrastructure is in place so that the team can work with maximum efficiency) ☐ ☐ ☐
    f) Linking (coordinating all work roles to ensure maximum cooperation and interchange of ideas, expertise, and experience) ☐ ☐ ☐
    Comments: _____
    _____

4. Who will be the spokesperson and chief contact for the institution on the project? It is *vital* that only one person speak for the institution during all the stages of the building process. _____

    _____

    Comments: _____

    _____

5. How will conflict be resolved on the project? _____

    _____

    Comments: _____

    _____

6. Who will make the final decision on design, space allocations, costs, and change orders? _____

    _____

    Comments: _____

    _____

C. Determining Space Needs

1. Has the library staff and administration met to decide the mission and long-term vision of the library? Space allocations and needs should be based on the vision and mission of the library.   ☐   ☐   ☐

    Comments: _____

    _____

2. What is the useful life of the new building? If it is an interim solution, how will this impact future needs?

    _____

    Comments: _____

    _____

3. What existing programs will be discontinued in the new building? _____

    _____

    Comments: _____

    _____

4. What new programs will be added in the new building? _____

    _____

    Comments: _____

    _____

5. What will be the growth of staff over the next twenty years? _____

    _____

    Comments: _____

    _____

                                                                          YES   NO   N/A

6.   What changes will take place in the service population over the next twenty years? _____

     _____

     Comments: _____

     _____

7.   What will be the growth of the collection over the next twenty years? _____

     _____

     Comments: _____

     _____

8.   What technology will be required to support library programs over the next twenty years? _____

     _____

     Comments: _____

     _____

9.   In estimating the size of the new building, have all of the following four factors been considered?

     a) "Building up" library spaces based on the programs and activities that the
        library wants to undertake in the new building. The total of all spaces equals
        the ideal size of the new building or expansion.   ☐   ☐   ☐

     b) The size of library buildings in similar institutions. It is valuable to have a
        database of ten similar libraries that may be consulted not only for facility size
        but also for other measurable aspects of library space. If you can't measure it,
        you can't manage it.   ☐   ☐   ☐

     c) Recommendations for space based on library association, regional, state, and
        other guidelines and standards   ☐   ☐   ☐

     d) Budget. This sometimes is the deciding factor.   ☐   ☐   ☐

     Comments: _____

     _____

10. Has a library building consultant been hired to help the library with planning?   ☐   ☐   ☐

     Comments: _____

     _____

11. Has a building program been prepared detailing space needs, adjacencies,
     and unique functions and features of the proposed building?   ☐   ☐   ☐

     Comments: _____

     _____

12. Has the library building consultant prepared the program or advised staff
     on preparing the program?   ☐   ☐   ☐

     Comments: _____

     _____

13. What will be the growth of seating requirements over the next twenty years? _____

     _____

     Comments: _____

     _____

YES   NO   N/A

14. Have the Association of College and Research Libraries Standards for Libraries in Higher Education (www.ala.org/ ala/mgrps/divs/acrl/standards/standardslibraries.cfm) been consulted? The ACRL document asks these questions about facilities:

a) Does the library provide well-planned, secure, and sufficient space to meet the perceived needs of staff and users?   ☐   ☐   ☐

b) Are building mechanical systems properly designed and maintained to control temperature and humidity at recommended levels?   ☐   ☐   ☐

c) What are the perceptions of users regarding the provision of conducive study spaces, including a sufficient number of seats and varied types of seating? _____

_____

d) Is there enough space for current library collections and future growth of print resources?   ☐   ☐   ☐

e) Does the staff have sufficient work space, and is it configured to promote efficient operations for current and future needs?   ☐   ☐   ☐

f) Does the library's signage facilitate use and navigation of the facilities?   ☐   ☐   ☐

g) Does the library provide ergonomic workstations for its users and staff?   ☐   ☐   ☐

h) Are electrical and network wiring sufficient to meet the needs associated with electronic access?   ☐   ☐   ☐

i) Does the library meet the requirements of the Americans with Disabilities Act (ADA)?   ☐   ☐   ☐

j) Are facilities provided to distance learners considered in the context of ACRL's Standards for Distance Learning Library Services (www.ala.org/ala/ mgrps/divs/acrl/standards/guidelinesdistancelearning.cfm)?   ☐   ☐   ☐

Comments: _____

_____

15. Has the ACRL/LAMA Guide for Architects, Guide for Planning Higher Education Library Spaces (http://wikis.ala.org/acrl/index.php/ACRL/LAMA_ Guide_for_Architects), been consulted?   ☐   ☐   ☐

Comments: _____

_____

16. Have Public Library Association planning documents been consulted? In particular:

a) *Public Library Service Responses, 2007:* These eighteen service responses update the original thirteen that appeared in the 1998 *Planning for Results: A Public Library Transformation Process.* Each service response contains eight sections: the title, the description, suggested target audiences, typical services and programs in libraries that select this as a priority, potential partners, policy implications, critical resources, and possible measures. Each of the service responses also suggests physical needs required to provide the response.   ☐   ☐   ☐

b) The 196 *Interim Standards for Small Public Libraries:* These standards have never been rescinded and are the only standards that recommend quantitative measures for public library size: 0.07 sq. ft./capita.   ☐   ☐   ☐

	YES	NO	N/A

c) *Managing Facilities for Results: Optimizing Space for Services* by Cheryl Bryan: This book dovetails with the basics outlined in *The New Planning for Results: A Streamlined Approach* to help public libraries plan physical spaces. ☐ ☐ ☐

Comments: _____

_____

17. Have the following sources for school library media centers been consulted?

a) The American Association of School Librarians has many excellent facilities planning suggestions on its website: www.ala.org/ala/mgrps/divs/ aasl/index.cfm. ☐ ☐ ☐

b) Rolf Erikson and Carolyn Markuson, *Designing a School Library Media Center for the Future*. This book will help school librarians anticipate needs and participate in the planning process with the architect, consultant(s), building committee, and administrators. ☐ ☐ ☐

c) Thomas L. Hart, *The School Library Media Facilities Planner*. This book is full of suggestions for all stages of the facility planning process, whether new construction or remodeling. The book shows exemplary facilities along with success stories and problems encountered. It includes a glossary and appendixes with model policies and planning documents. A companion DVD takes the viewer on tours of several new or remodeled school libraries. ☐ ☐ ☐

Comments: _____

_____

18. Has LAMA's *Building Blocks for Library Space* been consulted? This is a great source for specifying spaces required for library furniture and equipment. ☐ ☐ ☐

Comments: _____

_____

19. Has the California State Library's Libris Design Planning Documentation website been consulted (www.librisdesign.org/docs/index.html)? Libris Design is a library facility–planning database that assists local library officials with the planning of public library buildings. It includes a website with recent information on facility planning topics, a database of recently constructed California public libraries, an area for users to communicate with one another, user help documentation, and a trial version of the Libris Design database. ☐ ☐ ☐

Comments: _____

_____

D. Joint Use Considerations

1. Is there another organization on the campus or in the community that may offer synergy to the library by sharing facilities? ☐ ☐ ☐

Comments: _____

_____

	YES	NO	N/A

2. Is there another library or other organization that may offer potential synergy for a joint use facility? ☐ ☐ ☐

   Comments: _____

   _____

3. Do the missions of the libraries considering a joint facility have enough in common to enhance the chances of success? ☐ ☐ ☐

   Comments: _____

   _____

4. Are there possible efficiency and cost savings from having a joint facility? ☐ ☐ ☐

   Comments: _____

   _____

5. Can the quality and quantity of service be improved for both libraries through a joint facility? ☐ ☐ ☐

   Comments: _____

   _____

6. If a joint facility is selected, has a joint interagency agreement been negotiated? Some factors to be considered in the agreement are the following:

   a) *Governance.* A written agreement is strongly recommended, and it should list the parties entering into the agreement. The agreement should provide a clear demarcation of responsibility. ☐ ☐ ☐

   b) *Funding.* It is important to determine and put into an agreement the financial responsibilities of each party. This includes both capital and operational costs. ☐ ☐ ☐

   c) *Ownership of assets.* The agreement should clarify the ownership of assets brought into the shared library (such as equipment, collection, etc.) and how ownership will be determined in the event of termination of the combined library agreement. ☐ ☐ ☐

   d) *Hours of operation.* The agreement should list the hours of operation of both libraries and whether either partner has restrictions on use. ☐ ☐ ☐

   e) *Staffing.* Because a combined library is two libraries sharing one facility, it is recommended that local staffing requirements for both types of libraries be met. The two staffs may have different certification or licensing requirements. ☐ ☐ ☐

   f) *Volunteers.* Some libraries rely on youth and parent volunteers, and the other library may not use as many volunteers, if any. ☐ ☐ ☐

   g) *Collections.* Care must be taken to develop collections that are responsive to the needs of both sets of users. ☐ ☐ ☐

   h) *Changes.* How will changes in any of the above policies be determined? The agreement must be flexible enough to allow modifications as conditions change. ☐ ☐ ☐

   i) *Termination of the agreement.* If for some reason a termination is desired in the future, the agreement should state the conditions related to such termination. ☐ ☐ ☐

   Comments: _____

   _____

YES   NO   N/A

E. Alternatives to New Construction

1. Has the collection been weeded to eliminate unneeded books and media that take up space in the library?

   Comments: _____

   _____

2. Has the library's programming been reviewed, and programs eliminated that are no longer required and that take up space in the library?

   Comments: _____

   _____

3. Is it possible to renovate and refurbish existing spaces (improving the quality of the spaces and the ability of their occupants to work within them productively) in order to update spaces for electronics, better customer service, and atmosphere?

   Comments: _____

   _____

4. Is it possible to install high-density stacks to provide more book storage within the same book stack floor space area?

   Comments: _____

   _____

5. Has the library investigated a storage facility for low-use books and journals, and other little-used media and archival materials?

   Comments: _____

   _____

6. Has the library investigated leased space for public and nonpublic sections and activities that could function effectively outside the library in another location?

   Comments: _____

   _____

7. Has the library investigated adjacent buildings that might be acquired in order to add square footage to the existing library?

   Comments: _____

   _____

8. Has the library investigated modular buildings and/or kiosks that might be acquired instead of new construction?

   Comments: _____

   _____

	YES	NO	N/A

F. Selecting a Library Building Consultant

1. Is there someone on staff who has the necessary planning knowledge and experience regarding the functional needs and requirements of library buildings? If not, a library building consultant should be retained.   ☐ ☐ ☐

   Comments: _____

2. Has the consultant been retained at the very start of the building planning process so that he or she can take part in every step of the project?   ☐ ☐ ☐

   Comments: _____

3. Is the consultant listed in the Library Consultants Directory Online (www.rburgin.com/libraryconsultants/)?   ☐ ☐ ☐

   Comments: _____

4. Does the consultant have broad and diversified technical experience in planning new buildings, renovations and additions, and conversion of other buildings into library buildings?   ☐ ☐ ☐

   Comments: _____

5. Does the consultant have the organizational and record-keeping skills needed to document and respond to key events and activities during the project?   ☐ ☐ ☐

   Comments: _____

6. Does the consultant have the personal characteristics, experience, and skills necessary to assist a library in its unique planning and building needs?   ☐ ☐ ☐

   Comments: _____

7. Does the consultant have the written and verbal communication skills required to interact with all stakeholders?   ☐ ☐ ☐

   Comments: _____

8. Does the consultant have the political skills necessary to listen and respond to the concerns of all who may have a stake in the building project?   ☐ ☐ ☐

   Comments: _____

	YES	NO	N/A

9. Does the building consultant have the ability to explain a point of view and to persuade others of the importance of carrying out the consultant's recommendations? ☐ ☐ ☐

   Comments: _____

   _____

10. Will the consultant provide advice on the selection of the architect and other members of the building's technical planning team? ☐ ☐ ☐

    Comments: _____

    _____

11. Is the consultant's schedule flexible enough for him or her to be available for meetings with the library's planning committee when required? ☐ ☐ ☐

    Comments: _____

    _____

12. Is the consultant available by telephone, mail, or electronic communication to answer questions and provide guidance when his or her physical presence is not required? ☐ ☐ ☐

    Comments: _____

    _____

G. Choosing an Architect

1. Does the library staff play a major role in selecting the architect? ☐ ☐ ☐

   Comments: _____

   _____

2. Has the group responsible for selection of the architect developed selection criteria? ☐ ☐ ☐

   Comments: _____

   _____

3. Does the architect selection process include the following?

   a) Announcement of the proposed project in an official publication used by the client organization or in the general press ☐ ☐ ☐

   b) Requests for proposals and/or information ☐ ☐ ☐

   c) Submittals by interested firms ☐ ☐ ☐

   d) Provision of standardized forms so that a uniform evaluation of firms may take place ☐ ☐ ☐

   e) Evaluation based on the selection criteria developed by the group responsible for selection of the architect ☐ ☐ ☐

   f) Interviews with the "short list" of firms that the selection group has decided best meet the selection criteria ☐ ☐ ☐

   g) Ranking of the top firms to identify the best-qualified firms ☐ ☐ ☐

	YES	NO	N/A

h) Selection of the top-ranked firm based on the interview discussions and the selection criteria ☐ ☐ ☐

i) Notification of unsuccessful firms, and a debriefing as to why they were not selected ☐ ☐ ☐

Comments: _____

_____

4. Although not necessarily recommended, does the selection process involve

a) Limited or open architectural competitions? ☐ ☐ ☐

b) Design/build competitions? ☐ ☐ ☐

c) Bidding among various competitors? ☐ ☐ ☐

Comments: _____

_____

5. Is the architectural firm an individual, a partnership, a corporation, or a joint venture? _____

_____

Comments: _____

_____

6. Will the person who presents for the architectural team be involved in the project? ☐ ☐ ☐

Comments: _____

_____

7. Who will be in charge of designing the project? _____

_____

Comments: _____

_____

8. Who will supervise the project from design to completion? _____

_____

Comments: _____

_____

9. Is the architect or architectural firm registered to practice in the state? ☐ ☐ ☐

Comments: _____

_____

10. Is the architect of record registered to practice in the state? ☐ ☐ ☐

Comments: _____

_____

11. Are all key personnel and subconsultants involved in the project from the architect's office identified? ☐ ☐ ☐

Comments: _____

_____

	YES	NO	N/A

12. Are the architect's support team members identified (the landscape architect, civil engineer, structural engineer, acoustic engineer, mechanical engineer, electrical engineer, ADA compliance officer, and any other key specialists involved in the project)? ☐ ☐ ☐

   Comments: _____

   _____

13. Are all members of the architect's support team part of the firm, or does the architect retain them as subconsultants?

   _____

   Comments: _____

   _____

14. Does the architect's organization provide enough resources for the project? ☐ ☐ ☐

   Comments: _____

   _____

15. Does the architect have experience working with public agencies? ☐ ☐ ☐

   Comments: _____

   _____

16. Does the architect have prior experience in designing libraries? In some cases, it may be advantageous to have an architect who has not worked on a library building. ☐ ☐ ☐

   Comments: _____

   _____

17. If the architect has not worked with libraries, does he or she have a plan to become knowledgeable about library needs? This may require a library building consultant, preferably retained by the client. ☐ ☐ ☐

   Comments: _____

   _____

18. Is the architect an empathetic listener, willing to understand library needs? ☐ ☐ ☐

   Comments: _____

   _____

19. How will the architect gather information about library operations, the project site, and so forth? _____

   _____

   Comments: _____

   _____

20. What is the architect's design philosophy? _____

   Comments: _____

   _____

	YES	NO	N/A

21. Will the architect place library needs before design considerations? ☐ ☐ ☐

Comments: _____

_____

22. Does the architect's workload allow the firm to devote adequate time and energy to the project? ☐ ☐ ☐

Comments: _____

_____

23. Does the architect have solid reference reports from past clients? ☐ ☐ ☐

Comments: _____

_____

24. In projects completed by the architect:

   a) Did the projects come in at or under budget? ☐ ☐ ☐

   b) Did the projects come in on time? ☐ ☐ ☐

   c) What is the extent of change orders in number and dollars? _____

_____

   d) If there have been change orders, has it been determined whose fault they were? (Not all change orders are the architect's fault.) ☐ ☐ ☐

   e) What litigation has occurred against the architect? _____

_____

   f) What litigation has occurred against the architect's former clients by the architect? _____

_____

_____

Comments: _____

_____

25. Does the architect have written and verbal communication skills required for interacting with all stakeholders? ☐ ☐ ☐

Comments: _____

_____

26. Does the architect have the political skills necessary to listen and respond to the concerns of all external and internal building-project stakeholders? ☐ ☐ ☐

Comments: _____

_____

27. Does the architect have the ability to explain the reasons for a point of view and to persuade others of the importance of carrying out his or her recommendations? ☐ ☐ ☐

Comments: _____

_____

28. Does the architect's proposed fee fit into the fee guidelines of the American Institute of Architects? ☐ ☐ ☐

Comments: _____

_____

	YES	NO	N/A

29. Is the architect's proposed fee within the library's budget? ☐ ☐ ☐

    Comments: _____

_____

H. Choosing a Contractor

1. Will the award of the construction contract be made by a competitive bidding process? ☐ ☐ ☐

    Comments: _____

_____

2. Is a call or invitation to bid advertised in an official publication used by the client organization or in the general press? ☐ ☐ ☐

    Comments: _____

_____

3. For purposes of soliciting bids and awarding a contract, has the library declared who the "owner" is? (Usually the owner has legal and financial jurisdiction over the operations of the library.) ☐ ☐ ☐

    Comments: _____

_____

4. Does the bidding period extend for four to six weeks so that potential bidders may prepare their bids? ☐ ☐ ☐

    Comments: _____

_____

5. Are standardized bid forms provided so that a uniform evaluation of contractors may take place? ☐ ☐ ☐

    Comments: _____

_____

6. Are the architect and a library representative available to answer technical questions from potential bidders during the bid period? ☐ ☐ ☐

    Comments: _____

_____

7. Have a time and place been specified for opening bids? ☐ ☐ ☐

    Comments: _____

_____

8. During the bid opening, are all bids made public? ☐ ☐ ☐

    Comments: _____

_____

	YES	NO	N/A

9. After bids are received, are they "taken under advisement" by the owner so that the bids may be analyzed? ☐ ☐ ☐

   Comments: _____

   _____

10. During the bid analysis period, and before the contract is awarded, consider the following.

    a) Has the lowest bidder been checked for responsibility? ☐ ☐ ☐

    b) Is the submitted bid complete, accurate, and in compliance with the requirements, drawings, and specifications provided by the owner? ☐ ☐ ☐

    c) Does the contractor have sufficient staff to execute the scope of the project? ☐ ☐ ☐

    d) Has the contractor been in business long enough to establish a track record? ☐ ☐ ☐

    e) What references does the contractor provide? _____

    _____

    f) What is the contractor's record in successfully completing other projects? _____

    _____

    g) Does the contractor usually complete projects in the period specified? ☐ ☐ ☐

    h) Has any litigation occurred against the contractor? ☐ ☐ ☐

    i) What litigation has the contractor brought against previous clients and/or architects? _____

    _____

    j) What is the reputation of the subcontractors that the contractor has specified? _____

    _____

    k) Does the contractor have the necessary insurance and bonds to protect the owner as called for in the legal and financial specifications? ☐ ☐ ☐

    l) Does the contractor have the appropriate licenses to do the job? ☐ ☐ ☐

    Comments: _____

    _____

11. Is the bid awarded to the lowest responsible bidder? ☐ ☐ ☐

    Comments: _____

    _____

I. Architectural Design

1. Does the library design proposed by the architect meet the building program requirements? ☐ ☐ ☐

   Comments: _____

   _____

2. Does the design have the character and power to make the library building a focus for its community or campus? ☐ ☐ ☐

   Comments: _____

   _____

		YES	NO	N/A

3. Does the design take full advantage of all positive features of the site? ☐ ☐ ☐

   Comments: _____

   _____

4. Does the design compensate to the best degree possible for the negative aspects of the site? ☐ ☐ ☐

   Comments: _____

   _____

5. Is the architectural character distinctive in appearance, yet in harmony with its surroundings? ☐ ☐ ☐

   Comments: _____

   _____

6. Does the design welcome users and encourage nonusers to enter and investigate the library? ☐ ☐ ☐

   Comments: _____

   _____

7. Does the design create a building that is unmistakably public in character and function, yet very comfortable and nonintimidating for the user? ☐ ☐ ☐

   Comments: _____

   _____

8. Is the interior design in harmony with the exterior of the library? ☐ ☐ ☐

   Comments: _____

   _____

9. Do interior finishes create a space that is inviting to users, yet able to withstand the wear and tear of heavy public use? ☐ ☐ ☐

   Comments: _____

   _____

10. Does the design provide flexibility to take advantage of changes in library products and services, and roles and activities as well as technology? ☐ ☐ ☐

    Comments: _____

    _____

11. Does the design consider light, books, people, and the surrounding space as integral to one another? ☐ ☐ ☐

    Comments: _____

    _____

12. Does the design express symbolically the important values of knowledge and learning? ☐ ☐ ☐

    Comments: _____

    _____

	YES	NO	N/A

13. Does the design "sell" the products and services of the library by incorporating design features used successfully in retail merchandising? ☐ ☐ ☐

   Comments: _____

   _____

14. Does the design solve the paradoxical needs within a library for spatial openness and seclusion by creating the following?

   a) The ability to orient oneself within the visible total enclosure yet feel anchored to a particular part of it ☐ ☐ ☐

   b) The possibility of easy supervision by staff without the sense of being left exposed in a large impersonal space ☐ ☐ ☐

   c) A gradation of different spaces within the library, ranging from open areas of public activity to alcoves of semiprivate activity ☐ ☐ ☐

   d) Areas that have a sense of intimacy within the overall public setting ☐ ☐ ☐

   e) A wide variety of reading areas so that users have many choices to fit their mood or reading environment needs ☐ ☐ ☐

   f) A clear understanding upon entry to the library (and while moving within the library) of the general purpose of each library area ☐ ☐ ☐

   g) Clearly visible staff areas as a means for bringing information, services, and people together ☐ ☐ ☐

   Comments: _____

   _____

15. Does the library design plan encourage efficient traffic patterns from outside the structure into the building? ☐ ☐ ☐

   Comments: _____

   _____

16. Does the library design plan encourage efficient traffic patterns within the building? ☐ ☐ ☐

   Comments: _____

   _____

17. Does the library design provide for the maximum use of self-service by the library's customers? ☐ ☐ ☐

   Comments: _____

   _____

18. Does the design reflect the unique natural climate of the region where the library is located? ☐ ☐ ☐

   Comments: _____

   _____

19. Are windows treated or shaded to prevent the hot and damaging rays of the sun from penetrating the interiors? ☐ ☐ ☐

   Comments: _____

   _____

	YES	NO	N/A

20. Does the design provide flexibility in the placement of lighting fixtures, air ducts and registers, electrical power, and communication linkages to provide long-term flexibility?   ☐   ☐   ☐

Comments: _____

_____

21. Does the spacing of columns, shafts, and other architectural elements provide flexibility and the effective use of space?   ☐   ☐   ☐

Comments: _____

_____

22. Does the modular system employed meet the unique space needs of the library?   ☐   ☐   ☐

Comments: _____

_____

Library Site Selection

	YES	NO	N/A

A. General Conditions

1. Is the site conveniently located to the population served by the library? ☐ ☐ ☐
   Comments: _____

   _____

2. Does the site provide high visibility and identification to the population served? ☐ ☐ ☐
   Comments: _____

   _____

3. Is the site affordable? ☐ ☐ ☐
   Comments: _____

   _____

4. Will the site provide visibility of the building and its function from the street? ☐ ☐ ☐
   Comments: _____

   _____

5. Is a library an appropriate use of the land parcel in question? ☐ ☐ ☐
   Comments: _____

   _____

6. Will the site retain or enhance the natural contours of the land? ☐ ☐ ☐
   Comments: _____

   _____

		YES	NO	N/A

7. Is the site zoned for a library? ☐ ☐ ☐

    Comments: _____

_____

8. If not, is future library zoning possible? ☐ ☐ ☐

    Comments: _____

_____

9. Are there existing structures on the site that must be demolished? ☐ ☐ ☐

    Comments: _____

_____

10. If an existing structure must be demolished, does it present asbestos, lead paint, or unusual environmental problems? ☐ ☐ ☐

    Comments: _____

_____

11. If the library is to be a branch of a public library system, are there overlapping service areas from other branches in the system? ☐ ☐ ☐

    Comments: _____

_____

12. If the library is to be a branch of a college or university system, does the site provide ease of access for communication, transportation, and supply to the branch from other library service points? ☐ ☐ ☐

    Comments: _____

_____

13. Will the use of the site for a library add aesthetic value or other amenities to the neighborhood? ☐ ☐ ☐

    Comments: _____

_____

14. Are there liabilities or nuisance factors from adjacent properties and their activities? ☐ ☐ ☐

    Comments: _____

_____

15. Will the use of the site for a library have any negative impact on the surrounding areas? ☐ ☐ ☐

    Comments: _____

_____

16. Will the library fit in with the architectural style of neighboring buildings? ☐ ☐ ☐

    Comments: _____

_____

17. Will the building work with the traffic flow of adjacent areas? ☐ ☐ ☐

    Comments: _____

_____

	YES	NO	N/A

B. Location

1. Does the population being served consider the location of the site satisfactory and acceptable?   ☐ ☐ ☐

    Comments: _____

    _____

2. Is the site accessible to all segments of the community being served?   ☐ ☐ ☐

    Comments: _____

    _____

3. Is the site relatively close to the part of the community that is understood to be the most active and that will generate the most use?   ☐ ☐ ☐

    Comments: _____

    _____

4. Is the site appropriate for the library given its function and clientele?   ☐ ☐ ☐

    Comments: _____

    _____

5. Would library usage

    a) Increase if another site were selected?   ☐ ☐ ☐

    b) Decrease if another site were selected?   ☐ ☐ ☐

    c) Stay the same if another site were selected?   ☐ ☐ ☐

    Comments: _____

    _____

6. Will this location best meet the library objective of providing materials and services to the greatest number of people at the lowest cost?   ☐ ☐ ☐

    Comments: _____

    _____

7. Is the location in an area that is frequently visited by members of the community for daily activities such as going to class, shopping, working, and seeking out other services?   ☐ ☐ ☐

    Comments: _____

    _____

8. Is the site located near commercial, retail, cultural, and other activities within the community?   ☐ ☐ ☐

    Comments: _____

    _____

9. Does the proposed site present a safety issue for patrons and library staff?   ☐ ☐ ☐

    Comments: _____

    _____

	YES	NO	N/A

10. For public libraries, is the choice of location driven by the same factors that influence retail site selection? (A good rule of thumb is to get the site on the opposite corner from a McDonald's.)   ☐ ☐ ☐

Comments: _____

_____

C. Accessibility

1. Is the site easily accessible to those living in the area served?   ☐ ☐ ☐

Comments: _____

_____

2. For academic libraries, is the library located to best serve the interests and unique needs of the college or university?   ☐ ☐ ☐

A number of factors should be considered:

- For many institutions, the library is located in the center of the campus in order to link parts of the campus together. Most academic libraries are considered the heart of the campus, and the preferred location might be in the center of the campus.

- Libraries that serve primarily a commuter population might want to locate the library building near the transportation hub.

- Because the library needs to serve the entire population of the campus, it might be located at a site convenient to most classrooms.

- If departmental or special subject libraries exist, the library site's relationship to the other libraries might need to be considered.

Comments: _____

_____

3. For school libraries, the following accessibility factors should be considered. Is the library close to

   a) The study hall, to permit easy entry and return of students?   ☐ ☐ ☐

   b) The theater or auditorium, to provide good access to projection and taping equipment and to other graphic and audiovisual support services?   ☐ ☐ ☐

   c) A computer laboratory, to permit access to additional computers and peripheral equipment?   ☐ ☐ ☐

   d) The teacher workroom, to encourage teachers to use the center and to put equipment and resources within reach?   ☐ ☐ ☐

   e) The outside, to permit easy delivery of materials and after-hours access?   ☐ ☐ ☐

   Comments: _____

   _____

4. Can the greatest number of potential customers easily reach the site?   ☐ ☐ ☐

   Comments: _____

   _____

	YES	NO	N/A

5. Are travel times from target population areas to the library acceptable? ☐ ☐ ☐

Comments: _____

_____

6. Have automobile traffic patterns near the library been considered? ☐ ☐ ☐

Comments: _____

_____

7. Is the site located on a busy highway that will require a separate street-type entrance or driveway? ☐ ☐ ☐

Comments: _____

_____

8. Is the site accessible to public transportation? ☐ ☐ ☐

Comments: _____

_____

9. Is bicycle access encouraged and facilitated? ☐ ☐ ☐

Comments: _____

_____

10. Are there sidewalks for pedestrian access? ☐ ☐ ☐

Comments: _____

_____

11. Is the site conveniently accessible to private vehicle transportation? ☐ ☐ ☐

Comments: _____

_____

12. Does the entrance to the library provide adequate space and ease of accessibility to accommodate all arriving individuals and groups at all times? ☐ ☐ ☐

Comments: _____

_____

D. Size

1. Does the site provide adequate space for current needs? ☐ ☐ ☐

Comments: _____

_____

2. Will the site provide room for future expansion and/or remodeling? ☐ ☐ ☐

Comments: _____

_____

3. Does the site include enough space for appropriate amenities such as green space and landscaping? ☐ ☐ ☐

Comments: _____

_____

		YES	NO	N/A

4. Is the site large enough to accommodate on-site parking?   ☐   ☐   ☐

   Comments: _____

   _____

5. Does the property contain possible easements that may influence the type of
   construction that may take place on the site?   ☐   ☐   ☐

   Comments: _____

   _____

6. Does the property accommodate adequate setbacks to meet zoning and aesthetic
   considerations?   ☐   ☐   ☐

   Comments: _____

   _____

7. Is the property configuration adequate for successful completion of the building
   project?   ☐   ☐   ☐

   Comments: _____

   _____

8. Is there enough space on the property and/or adjacent to it for staging during
   construction?   ☐   ☐   ☐

   Comments: _____

   _____

E. Environmental Issues

1. Has an environmental impact report been made for the proposed site?   ☐   ☐   ☐

   Comments: _____

   _____

2. Is the site oriented so that it is possible to take advantage of solar energy and/or
   photovoltaic (PV) systems?   ☐   ☐   ☐

   Comments: _____

   _____

3. Are complications likely to arise from the nature of the ground beneath the
   building?   ☐   ☐   ☐

   Comments: _____

   _____

4. Does the site have adequate drainage?   ☐   ☐   ☐

   Comments: _____

   _____

		YES	NO	N/A

5. Is the site above the level of a 100-year flood plain? ☐ ☐ ☐

Comments: _____

_____

6. Has a subsurface probe been done to examine soil conditions, utilities, and other factors? ☐ ☐ ☐

Comments: _____

_____

7. Has the site been improved—that is, are curbs, gutters, water, sewers, and electricity available? ☐ ☐ ☐

Comments: _____

_____

8. Are there any natural or artificial barriers that limit either access to or usability of the site? ☐ ☐ ☐

Comments: _____

_____

9. Are there any hidden problems of geology, topography, archaeology, buried objects, or toxic waste? ☐ ☐ ☐

Comments: _____

_____

10. Does the site present issues with indigenous peoples or endangered species? ☐ ☐ ☐

Comments: _____

_____

11. Do neighboring facilities pose possible environmental/nuisance problems? ☐ ☐ ☐

Comments: _____

_____

12. Has the condition of the soil been tested to determine the stability of the site or any underground site problems? ☐ ☐ ☐

Comments: _____

_____

13. If the site is sloped, are there possible advantages or disadvantages to the slope? ☐ ☐ ☐

Comments: _____

_____

Sustainable Design

	YES	NO	N/A

Many of the following checklist items are adapted from the U.S. Green Building Council recommendations.

A. Sustainable Sites

1. Is the new building or renovation designed and constructed in ways that preserve the natural outdoor environment and promote a healthful indoor habitat? ☐ ☐ ☐

   Comments: _____

   _____

2. Is the building project designed to avoid an adverse impact on the natural state of the air, land, and water by using resources and methods that minimize pollution and waste and that do not cause permanent damage to the earth, including erosion? ☐ ☐ ☐

   Comments: _____

   _____

3. Is the building designed to take the maximum advantage of passive and natural sources of heat, cooling, ventilation, and light? ☐ ☐ ☐

   Comments: _____

   _____

4. Are innovative strategies and technologies, such as porous paving to conserve water and reduce effluent and runoff, employed? ☐ ☐ ☐

   Comments: _____

   _____

	YES	NO	N/A

5. Is the project planned to reduce the need for individual automobiles, to use alternative fuels, and to encourage public and alternative modes of transportation such as bicycles? ☐ ☐ ☐

   Comments: _____

_____

6. Is it possible to locate the library within one-half mile of an existing (or planned and funded) commuter rail, light rail, or subway station? ☐ ☐ ☐

   Comments: _____

_____

7. Does the building provide secure bicycle racks and/or storage within 200 yards of a building entrance? ☐ ☐ ☐

   Comments: _____

_____

8. Are there shower and changing facilities in the building, or within 200 yards of a building entrance? (Such facilities will be appreciated by bicycle commuters and will gain points in the LEED rating.) ☐ ☐ ☐

   Comments: _____

_____

9. Does the library provide preferred parking for low-emitting and hybrid fuel-efficient vehicles equal to 5 percent of the total vehicle parking capacity of the site, and at least one designated carpool drop-off area? ☐ ☐ ☐

   Comments: _____

_____

10. Is the library building planned for a sustainable site? ☐ ☐ ☐

    Some inappropriate sites include the following:

    - Prime farmland as defined by the U.S. Department of Agriculture
    - Previously undeveloped land whose elevation is lower than 5 feet above the elevation of the 100-year flood plain as defined by FEMA (Federal Emergency Management Agency)
    - Land that is specifically identified as habitat for any species on federal or state threatened or endangered lists
    - Land within 100 feet of any wetlands as defined by the U.S. Code of Federal Regulations
    - Previously undeveloped land that is within 50 feet of a water body, defined as seas, lakes, rivers, streams, and tributaries that support or could support fish, recreation, or industrial use, consistent with the terminology of the Clean Water Act
    - Land that prior to acquisition for the project was public parkland, unless land of equal or greater value as parkland is accepted in trade by the public landowner

    Comments: _____

_____

	YES	NO	N/A

11. Is it possible for the library site to rehabilitate damaged sites where development is complicated by environmental contamination, thereby reducing pressure on undeveloped land? ☐ ☐ ☐

    Comments: _____

    _____

12. Do greenfield sites limit all site disturbances to the least possible area beyond the building perimeter? (Greenfield sites are areas of land that have not previously been built on and that might well be put to agricultural or amenity use. Sites that have been previously built on and that have been or can be cleared for redevelopment are referred to as brownfield sites.) ☐ ☐ ☐

    Comments: _____

    _____

13. On previously developed or graded brownfield sites, is it possible to restore the site with native or adapted vegetation? ☐ ☐ ☐

    Comments: _____

    _____

14. Is it possible to reduce the development footprint (defined as the total area of the building footprint, hardscape, access roads, and parking) and/or provide vegetated open space within the project boundary to exceed the local zoning code's open space requirement for the site? ☐ ☐ ☐

    Comments: _____

    _____

15. Is it possible to implement a stormwater management plan that reduces impervious cover, promotes infiltration, and captures and treats the stormwater runoff from 90 percent of the average annual rainfall using acceptable best management practices (BMPs)? ☐ ☐ ☐

    Comments: _____

    _____

16. To lessen the impact on microclimates and on human and wildlife habitats, can heat islands (thermal gradient differences between developed and undeveloped areas) be minimized through shade, paving materials, and an open-grid pavement system? ☐ ☐ ☐

    Comments: _____

    _____

17. Can roofing materials and/or a vegetated roof be used to reduce thermal heat islands? ☐ ☐ ☐

    Comments: _____

    _____

18. Can the light trespass from the building and site be minimized to reduce sky glow to increase night sky access, improve nighttime visibility through glare reduction, and reduce development impact on nocturnal environments? ☐ ☐ ☐

    Comments: _____

    _____

	YES	NO	N/A

19. Is it possible to make the library a more integrated part of the community by enabling the building and its grounds to be used for nonlibrary events and functions? ☐ ☐ ☐

Comments: _____

_____

B. Water Efficiency

1. Is only captured rainwater, recycled wastewater, recycled gray water, or water treated and conveyed by a public agency specifically for nonpotable uses employed for irrigation? ☐ ☐ ☐

Comments: _____

_____

2. Has landscaping (native plants) been installed that does not require permanent irrigation systems? Temporary irrigation systems used for plant establishment should be removed within one year of installation. Native plants in a particular area are those that were growing naturally in the area before humans introduced plants from distant places. ☐ ☐ ☐

Comments: _____

_____

3. Has potable water use for building sewage conveyance been reduced by installing water-conserving fixtures (water closets, urinals) or using nonpotable water (captured rainwater, recycled gray water, and on-site or municipally treated wastewater)? ☐ ☐ ☐

Comments: _____

_____

4. Are high-efficiency fixtures and dry fixtures such as composting toilet systems and non-water-using urinals used to reduce wastewater? ☐ ☐ ☐

Comments: _____

_____

5. Has reuse of stormwater and gray water for nonpotable applications such as toilet and urinal flushing, mechanical systems, and custodial uses been considered? ☐ ☐ ☐

Comments: _____

_____

6. Has refrigeration equipment using once-through cooling with potable water not been used? Not using this type of system increases water efficiency and reduces the burden on the municipal water supply and wastewater systems. ☐ ☐ ☐

Comments: _____

_____

                                                           YES   NO   N/A

C. Energy and Atmosphere

1. Are the building envelope and systems designed to maximize energy performance?   ☐   ☐   ☐
    Comments: _____
    _____

2. Has a computer simulation model been used to assess the energy performance
    and to identify the most cost-effective energy efficiency measures?   ☐   ☐   ☐
    Comments: _____
    _____

3. Have on-site renewable energy systems been employed to offset building energy
    costs?   ☐   ☐   ☐
    Comments: _____
    _____

4. Can all or part of the energy needs of the building be met by green power? Green
    power is derived from solar, wind, geothermal, biomass, or low-impact hydro sources.   ☐   ☐   ☐
    Comments: _____
    _____

5. Are the building's energy-related systems regularly inspected, calibrated, and
    verified to determine that they perform according to the installed requirements,
    basis of design, and construction documents?   ☐   ☐   ☐
    Comments: _____
    _____

6. Have refrigerants and HVAC&R (Heating, Ventilating, Air-Conditioning, and
    Refrigerating) systems been selected that minimize or eliminate the emission of
    compounds that contribute to ozone depletion and global warming?   ☐   ☐   ☐
    Comments: _____
    _____

7. Is there zero use of CFC-based refrigerants in the building's HVAC&R systems?   ☐   ☐   ☐
    Comments: _____
    _____

8. Are there fire suppression systems that contain ozone-depleting substances
    (CFCs, HCFCs, or halons)? Substitutes might be a fire detection system and
    a zoned sprinkler system.   ☐   ☐   ☐
    Comments: _____
    _____

9. Have photovoltaic cells been planned to help generate electricity? Photovoltaic
    cells convert light into electricity at the atomic level. A cost-benefit analysis
    should be done to determine the economic benefits of photovoltaics.   ☐   ☐   ☐
    Comments: _____
    _____

YES   NO   N/A

D. Materials

1. In planning for a new library building, has the reuse of existing buildings, including structure, envelope, and interior nonstructural elements, been considered? ☐ ☐ ☐

   Comments: _____

   _____

2. Has construction, demolition, and land-clearing debris been diverted from disposal in landfills and incinerators to recycling? (Redirect recyclable recovered resources back to the manufacturing process. Redirect reusable materials to appropriate sites.) ☐ ☐ ☐

   Comments: _____

   _____

3. Have opportunities to incorporate salvaged materials into building design been considered and potential material suppliers been researched? (Salvaged materials such as beams and posts, flooring, paneling, doors and frames, cabinetry and furniture, brick, and decorative items should be considered.) ☐ ☐ ☐

   Comments: _____

   _____

4. Have materials with recycled content been considered for use in new construction? ☐ ☐ ☐

   Comments: _____

   _____

5. Is the building constructed and operated using materials, methods, and mechanical and electrical systems that ensure a healthful indoor air quality, while avoiding contamination by carcinogens, volatile organic compounds, fungi, molds, bacteria, and other known toxins? ☐ ☐ ☐

   Comments: _____

   _____

6. Are copy rooms and similar spaces that emit possibly toxic substances equipped with their own dedicated air exhaust systems? ☐ ☐ ☐

   Comments: _____

   _____

7. Are particleboards that emit formaldehyde prohibited in the building? ☐ ☐ ☐

   Comments: _____

   _____

8. Are only solvent-free paints specified for the project? ☐ ☐ ☐

   Comments: _____

   _____

9. Are low-emitting, solvent-free adhesives specified for the project? ☐ ☐ ☐

   Comments: _____

   _____

	YES	NO	N/A
10. Is furniture constructed without particleboards that emit formaldehyde?	☐	☐	☐

Comments: _____

11. In evaluating the environmental performance of materials used in the building, have the following been considered?

	YES	NO	N/A
a) Energy efficient and with low embodied energy	☐	☐	☐
b) Made of renewable materials	☐	☐	☐
c) Made of postconsumer recycled materials	☐	☐	☐
d) Made of postindustrial recycled materials	☐	☐	☐
e) Made of certified wood	☐	☐	☐
f) Healthy for indoor air—low VOC	☐	☐	☐
g) Healthy for the atmosphere—no CFCs or HCFCs used in manufacturing	☐	☐	☐
h) Nontoxic in use, production, or at end of useful life	☐	☐	☐
i) Made of salvaged materials	☐	☐	☐
j) Recyclable at end of useful life	☐	☐	☐
k) Simple to install without dangerous adhesives, etc.	☐	☐	☐
l) Made near the building site—low transportation impacts	☐	☐	☐
m) Efficient/resourceful/reusable packaging	☐	☐	☐

Comments: _____

	YES	NO	N/A
12. Is there a project goal for locally sourced materials, and have those materials and material suppliers that can achieve this goal been identified?	☐	☐	☐

Comments: _____

	YES	NO	N/A
13. Have rapidly renewable building materials and products (made from plants that are typically harvested within a ten-year cycle or shorter) been specified? Consider materials such as bamboo, wool, cotton insulation, agrifiber, linoleum, wheatboard, strawboard, and cork.	☐	☐	☐

Comments: _____

	YES	NO	N/A
14. Is there an easily accessible area that serves the entire building and is dedicated to the collection and storage of nonhazardous materials for recycling, including (at a minimum) paper, corrugated cardboard, glass, plastics, and metals?	☐	☐	☐

Comments: _____

E. Indoor Environmental Air Quality

	YES	NO	N/A
1. Is smoking prohibited in the building?	☐	☐	☐

Comments: _____

	YES	NO	N/A

2. Are any exterior designated smoking areas at least 25 feet away from entries, outdoor-air intakes, and operable windows? ☐ ☐ ☐

   Comments: _____

   _____

3. Is there a permanent monitoring system that provides feedback on ventilation system performance to ensure that ventilation systems maintain design minimum ventilation requirements? ☐ ☐ ☐

   Comments: _____

   _____

4. Is there a building "flushout" after construction ends and prior to occupancy and after all interior finishes are installed? A building flushout is performed by supplying a total air volume of 14,000 cubic feet of outdoor air per square foot of floor area while maintaining an internal temperature of at least 60 degrees Fahrenheit and relative humidity no higher than 60 percent. ☐ ☐ ☐

   Comments: _____

   _____

5. Are carbon dioxide concentrations within all densely occupied spaces (those with a design occupant density greater than or equal to twenty-five people per 1,000 square feet) monitored? CO_2 monitoring locations should be between 3 feet and 6 feet above the floor. ☐ ☐ ☐

   Comments: _____

   _____

6. Are any sources of chemicals that could be hazardous to occupants isolated? This may include separating copiers into spaces that can be properly ventilated so that the ozone from the copiers does not affect the entire library. This will also include keeping the pollutants from the streets, sidewalks, and parking lots out of the library by having effective walk-off mats at all main entryways. ☐ ☐ ☐

   Comments: _____

   _____

7. Are the HVAC&R system's outdoor-air intakes located as high as possible above the ground and far enough away from the exhaust ducts to reduce the intake of ground-level air pollution (exhaust from traffic)? ☐ ☐ ☐

   Comments: _____

   _____

8. Are air filters designed to be easy to access and to clean and/or replace? ☐ ☐ ☐

   Comments: _____

   _____

9. Are stainless-steel-strip bird guards installed over the horizontal rooftop outdoor-air intakes to prevent birds from settling on the grating and polluting the shafts below? ☐ ☐ ☐

   Comments: _____

   _____

	YES	NO	N/A

10. Has the exposed fiberglass (porous insulation) within the HVAC&R system been encapsulated to eliminate amplification sites for fungal and bacterial microorganisms? ☐ ☐ ☐

   Comments: _____

   _____

11. Is the rate of ventilation with outdoor air at the rate of 25 cubic feet per minute? ☐ ☐ ☐

   Comments: _____

   _____

F. Lighting and Day Lighting

1. Is lighting used for

   a) Aesthetics to illuminate the exterior of the library and landscape? ☐ ☐ ☐

   b) Security to illuminate the grounds near the library, driveways, and parking areas? ☐ ☐ ☐

   c) Utility to illuminate the building, driveways, and parking areas to help people navigate safely to and from the library? ☐ ☐ ☐

   Comments: _____

   _____

2. Is day lighting used as a passive strategy to improve the indoor environmental quality of the library? ☐ ☐ ☐

   Comments: _____

   _____

3. If day lighting is used, is there a daylight sensor to control the lights in day-lit spaces? Using photosensors in day-lit spaces to control dimmable ballasts will allow a system to work without being actively operated by occupants. ☐ ☐ ☐

   Comments: _____

   _____

4. Is there a system to reduce the amount of time that lights are on? This can be accomplished by using dimmers and other lighting controls that turn off unneeded lights when a space is not occupied. ☐ ☐ ☐

   Comments: _____

   _____

5. Is wattage reduced by replacing bulbs or entire fixtures with bulbs and fixtures that provide the same amount or greater amounts of light but with reduced electricity usage? Today, this can be accomplished most easily by replacing inefficient incandescent bulbs with incandescent/halogen bulbs or compact fluorescent bulbs. ☐ ☐ ☐

   Comments: _____

   _____

YES   NO   N/A

G. Roofs

1. Has a green roof been considered? A green roof system is an extension of the existing roof and includes a high-quality waterproofing and root-repellant system, a drainage system, filter cloth, and lightweight, growing plants and vegetation. Green roof development involves the creation of "contained" green space on top of a human-made structure. This green space could be below, at, or above grade, but in all cases the plants are not planted in the ground. Green roofs can provide a wide range of public and private benefits.   ☐   ☐   ☐

   Comments: _____

   _____

2. If a green roof is not used, has a cool roof been considered? Cool roofs use materials that reflect the sun's energy and help keep the indoor temperature down, reducing the heat load and requirements on the cooling system in the warmer months. Reflective or light-colored roofing materials are particularly recommended in hot and humid environments.   ☐   ☐   ☐

   Comments: _____

   _____

3. Has a roof with a photovoltaic (PV) energy system been considered? Photovoltaic systems convert sunlight directly into electricity.   ☐   ☐   ☐

   Comments: _____

   _____

General Exterior Considerations

		YES	NO	N/A

A. Landscaping

1. Has the landscape design been considered early in the planning and design stage?   ☐ ☐ ☐
   Comments: _____

2. Has a landscape architect been retained as one of the architect's subconsultants?   ☐ ☐ ☐
   Comments: _____

3. Does the landscape design enhance the overall design of the building?   ☐ ☐ ☐
   Comments: _____

4. Does the landscaping complement and enhance the site and adjoining neighborhood?   ☐ ☐ ☐
   Comments: _____

5. Is the landscaping visually satisfying and inviting?   ☐ ☐ ☐
   Comments: _____

6. Is the landscaping design in harmony with the climatic zone of the library site?   ☐ ☐ ☐
   Comments: _____

	YES	NO	N/A

7. Has xeriscape been considered? ☐ ☐ ☐

Xeriscape is a combination of commonsense landscaping principles that save water while creating a lush and colorful landscape. It includes the following steps:

- Plan and design the landscape project.
- Create practical turf areas of manageable sizes, shapes, and appropriate grasses. Turf is used to enhance the landscaping and is used judiciously.
- Select and group plants appropriately. Different plants have different light, soil, and water requirements.
- Use soil amendments like compost or manure as needed by the site and the types of plants used.
- Use mulches such as woodchips to reduce evaporation and to keep the soil cool.
- Irrigate efficiently with properly designed systems (including hose-end equipment) and by applying the right amount of water at the right time.
- Maintain the landscaping by mowing, weeding, pruning, and fertilizing properly.

Comments: _____

_____

8. Do the plants selected provide pleasing colors and textures throughout all seasons of the year? ☐ ☐ ☐

Comments: _____

_____

9. Is the landscaping designed from both an interior and exterior perspective to enhance the experience when one looks toward the library and looks out from the library? ☐ ☐ ☐

Comments: _____

_____

10. Is there an adequate amount of good soil? ☐ ☐ ☐

Comments: _____

_____

11. Is there adequate drainage? ☐ ☐ ☐

Comments: _____

_____

12. Are the plants selected appropriate to the amount of sun and/or shade they will receive? ☐ ☐ ☐

Comments: _____

_____

13. Do trees and shrubs enhance the building's energy and water conservation efforts? ☐ ☐ ☐

Comments: _____

_____

14. Are the plants and shrubs selected not subject to damaging attacks by insects or disease? ☐ ☐ ☐

Comments: _____

_____

		YES	NO	N/A

15. Can the landscaping be easily and inexpensively maintained? ☐ ☐ ☐

   Comments: _____

   _____

16. Is there an automatic irrigation system in place? ☐ ☐ ☐

   Comments: _____

   _____

17. Is the parking area landscaped in conformance with local codes and regulations? ☐ ☐ ☐

   Comments: _____

   _____

18. Is a local garden club or community organization willing to provide volunteer gardening as a public service? ☐ ☐ ☐

   Comments: _____

   _____

B. Parking

1. Are there sufficient parking spaces for staff as well as customers during all service hours? ☐ ☐ ☐

   Comments: _____

   _____

2. Does the site provide adequate parking spaces to meet institutional and local parking codes? ☐ ☐ ☐

   Comments: _____

   _____

3. Do handicapped parking spaces meet or exceed ADA regulations in both number and specifications? ☐ ☐ ☐

   Comments: _____

   _____

4. Is parking convenient to the library's entrances? ☐ ☐ ☐

   Comments: _____

   _____

5. Is the parking area well lit at night? ☐ ☐ ☐

   Comments: _____

   _____

6. Is there adequate parking for large cars and trucks? ☐ ☐ ☐

   Comments: _____

   _____

7. If there is a parking garage, is it close to the library's main entrance? ☐ ☐ ☐

   Comments: _____

   _____

		YES	NO	N/A
8.	Is the parking garage well identified from the street?	☐	☐	☐
	Comments: _____			
9.	Is the parking garage secure and well lit at all times?	☐	☐	☐
	Comments: _____			
10.	Can cars easily get in and out of parking lots and/or structures?	☐	☐	☐
	Comments: _____			
11.	If the library has an employee recognition program, is there a designated parking space for "staffer of the month" very near the staff or receiving entrance?	☐	☐	☐
	Comments: _____			
12.	If there is a bookmobile, is parking convenient for staff to move materials on and off the vehicle?	☐	☐	☐
	Comments: _____			
13.	If there is a community room, is there adequate parking for the extra cars that will need to be accommodated?	☐	☐	☐
	Comments: _____			
14.	In northern climates, is there adequate room for snowplow access as well as snow stacking space?	☐	☐	☐
	Comments: _____			
15.	Does the library subsidize parking if free parking is not available?	☐	☐	☐
	Comments: _____			
16.	If the library parking is metered, does the library provide convenient coin-changing machines?	☐	☐	☐
	Comments: _____			
17.	If the library does not provide parking, is public parking available nearby?	☐	☐	☐
	Comments: _____			

		YES	NO	N/A

C. Building Exterior

1. Is the building aesthetically pleasing during the day and night? ☐ ☐ ☐
   Comments: _____
   _____

2. Is the fenestration arranged to take maximum advantage of natural light and the best views, while allowing use of floor and wall space inside the building? ☐ ☐ ☐
   Comments: _____
   _____

3. Will sunlight, glare, and excessive ultraviolet rays be controlled architecturally? ☐ ☐ ☐
   Comments: _____
   _____

4. Are all exterior architectural features and surfaces constructed of easily maintained materials? ☐ ☐ ☐
   Comments: _____
   _____

5. Do walls have a hard texture that is not easily scratched? ☐ ☐ ☐
   Comments: _____
   _____

6. Do walls have a graffiti-repellent coating? ☐ ☐ ☐
   Comments: _____
   _____

7. Do all exterior access walks and surfaces meet ADA requirements? ☐ ☐ ☐
   Comments: _____
   _____

8. Are all walkways and ramps leading into the building well lit? ☐ ☐ ☐
   Comments: _____
   _____

9. In northern areas, do sidewalk lamps give off heat to help melt snow and ice? ☐ ☐ ☐
   Comments: _____
   _____

10. Are walkway surfaces stable and firm? ☐ ☐ ☐
    Comments: _____
    _____

11. Are walkway surfaces slip-resistant? ☐ ☐ ☐
    Comments: _____
    _____

		YES	NO	N/A

12. Are stair steps uniform in height and width?   ☐   ☐   ☐

    Comments: _____

13. Is there a separate staff entrance?   ☐   ☐   ☐

    Comments: _____

14. Are public telephones available outside?   ☐   ☐   ☐

    Comments: _____

15. Is there provision for storage of lawn mowers, snowblowers, and other outside equipment?   ☐   ☐   ☐

    Comments: _____

16. Is there provision outside for vandal-proof faucets and electrical outlets?   ☐   ☐   ☐

    Comments: _____

D. Roof

1. In northern areas, is the roof peaked to facilitate drainage?   ☐   ☐   ☐

    Comments: _____

2. Are drainage systems on the roof adequate to carry off water from heavy downpours or melted snow?   ☐   ☐   ☐

    Comments: _____

3. Are the roof and eaves areas well insulated to allow for maximum energy efficiency?   ☐   ☐   ☐

    Comments: _____

4. Is it possible to walk on the roof safely and without damaging it?   ☐   ☐   ☐

    Comments: _____

5. Is the building's roof easily maintained?   ☐   ☐   ☐

    Comments: _____

6. Are entrances and walkways protected from avalanches of water, snow, or ice accumulated on the roof?   ☐   ☐   ☐

    Comments: _____

		YES	NO	N/A
7.	Do downspouts carry the water away from the building and sidewalks into storm drains?	☐	☐	☐

Comments: _____

_____

E. Bicycle Racks

1.	Are bicycle racks clearly visible from the street and/or interior?	☐	☐	☐

Comments: _____

_____

2.	Are bicycle racks convenient to the building entrances without being an obstacle for people entering the library?	☐	☐	☐

Comments: _____

_____

3.	Are bicycle racks equipped with locks?	☐	☐	☐

Comments: _____

_____

4.	Are the bicycle racks in a well-lit area?	☐	☐	☐

Comments: _____

_____

F. Flagpole

1.	Is there a flagpole outside the building?	☐	☐	☐

Comments: _____

_____

2. Is it a ground-set, wall-mounted, or roof-mounted pole? _____

_____

Comments: _____

_____

3.	Is there a self-storing flagpole shaft?	☐	☐	☐

Comments: _____

_____

4.	Can the flag be raised, lowered, and drawn into the pole either manually or electrically?	☐	☐	☐

Comments: _____

_____

5.	Is the flagpole safe from vandalism?	☐	☐	☐

Comments: _____

_____

	YES	NO	N/A

6. If the flag is to be flown at night, is it adequately lit? ☐ ☐ ☐

   Comments: _____

   _____

G. Exterior Signage

1. Is signage incorporated into the preliminary design of the site, parking areas, and building? ☐ ☐ ☐

   Comments: _____

   _____

2. Does signage comply with the Americans with Disabilities Act (ADA)? ☐ ☐ ☐

   Comments: _____

   _____

3. Is the standard international symbol for libraries displayed? ☐ ☐ ☐

   Comments: _____

   _____

4. Is there a large, exterior, well-lit sign identifying the library? ☐ ☐ ☐

   Comments: _____

   _____

5. Is the exterior sign clearly visible from passing cars during the day and night? ☐ ☐ ☐

   Comments: _____

   _____

6. Does the sign have space for advertising of library events, holiday hours, etc.? ☐ ☐ ☐

   Comments: _____

   _____

7. Are the library's hours of service prominently displayed on a large, well-lit sign at the entrance along with an OPEN/CLOSED sign? ☐ ☐ ☐

   Comments: _____

   _____

8. Do the colors of the letters contrast with the color of the sign and complement the outside of the building? ☐ ☐ ☐

   Comments: _____

   _____

9. Are signs attached to the wall adjacent to the latch side of the door? ☐ ☐ ☐

   Comments: _____

   _____

10. Would a map, directory, or graphic be more appropriate than a sign? ☐ ☐ ☐

    Comments: _____

    _____

	YES	NO	N/A

11. Do pictorial signs have verbal descriptions placed below the picture?   ☐ ☐ ☐
    Comments: _____
    _____

12. Are the letters in a sans serif or a simple serif type?   ☐ ☐ ☐
    Comments: _____
    _____

13. Do signs have a nonglare finish?   ☐ ☐ ☐
    Comments: _____
    _____

14. When selecting sign size, have background and distance been considered?   ☐ ☐ ☐
    Comments: _____
    _____

15. Is sign size 1 inch for every 50 feet of visibility and a minimum of 3 inches?   ☐ ☐ ☐
    Comments: _____
    _____

16. Has negative phrasing been avoided in signage?   ☐ ☐ ☐
    Comments: _____
    _____

17. Are the signs durable and can they be easily and cost-effectively replaced?   ☐ ☐ ☐
    Comments: _____
    _____

18. Are signs read horizontally and not vertically?   ☐ ☐ ☐
    Comments: _____
    _____

19. If there is an arrow to indicate direction, is it separate from the lettered sign so
    that it can be changed if necessary?   ☐ ☐ ☐
    Comments: _____
    _____

H. Loading Docks and Delivery

Many of these checklist items are from the Whole Building Design Guide website (www.wbdg.org/index.php).

1. Is the loading dock and/or delivery area clearly marked and easily accessible from
   the street?   ☐ ☐ ☐
   Comments: _____
   _____

2. Is there generous space for easy truck turnaround?   ☐ ☐ ☐
   Comments: _____
   _____

		YES	NO	N/A

3. Is there a buzzer and/or internal telephone at or near the delivery entrance?   ☐   ☐   ☐
    Comments: _____
    _____

4. If there is no loading dock, is parking for delivery vehicles located close to the exit nearest the delivery area or workroom?   ☐   ☐   ☐
    Comments: _____
    _____

5. Is the loading dock located away from the primary work and public areas so that noise and fumes do not disturb staff or users?   ☐   ☐   ☐
    Comments: _____
    _____

6. Is a ramp provided from the loading dock down to the truck parking area to facilitate deliveries from small trucks and vans? This ramp should have a maximum slope of 1:12 and comply with UFAS (Uniform Federal Accessibility Standards)/ADA Accessibility Guidelines ensuring that it may be easily traversed by carts and dollies.   ☐   ☐   ☐
    Comments: _____
    _____

7. Are the loading docks located for easy access by service vehicles and separated from public entrances to the building and from public spaces?   ☐   ☐   ☐
    Comments: _____
    _____

8. Are loading docks convenient to freight elevators so that service is segregated from the main passenger elevator lobbies and public corridors? The service route from the elevator should accommodate the transport of large items.   ☐   ☐   ☐
    Comments: _____
    _____

9. Are loading docks designed to accommodate vehicles used to deliver or pick up materials from the library? If the bed height of vans and trucks varies more than 18 inches, at least one loading berth should be equipped with a dock leveler. Typical docks are built 55 inches above grade level to accommodate most trucks.   ☐   ☐   ☐
    Comments: _____
    _____

10. Does the loading dock have a minimum overhead clearance of 14 feet?   ☐   ☐   ☐
    Comments: _____
    _____

11. Is each truck position equipped with adjustable lighting fixtures for the illumination of the interior of trailers?   ☐   ☐   ☐
    Comments: _____
    _____

	YES	NO	N/A

12. Are loading docks protected with edge guards and dock bumpers? ☐ ☐ ☐

Comments: _____

_____

13. Are easy-access, overhead coiling doors used for the loading docks? These doors should be able to close completely and lock after the loading docks are closed. At least one well-lit personnel door should be provided in addition to the overhead doors. ☐ ☐ ☐

Comments: _____

_____

14. Are noise mitigation strategies used? Noise reduction in the dock and noise transmission out of the dock are different design considerations. Mass and limpness/flexibility are two desirable attributes for a sound transmission barrier. Unpainted heavy masonry walls provide mass. Absorptive acoustical surfacing will reduce the noise level in the dock but will have little effect on the transmission outside it. Noise levels in the dock should be moderated to promote communication among users. ☐ ☐ ☐

Comments: _____

_____

15. Is resilient flooring used in offices adjacent to the loading docks? ☐ ☐ ☐

Comments: _____

_____

16. Is the truck's approach to the dock at grade or sloped away from the loading dock to prevent the collection of stormwater near the dock? ☐ ☐ ☐

Comments: _____

_____

17. Are loading docks covered at least 4 feet beyond the edge of the platform over the loading berth to protect users and goods being unloaded? ☐ ☐ ☐

Comments: _____

_____

18. Is a staging area inside the building provided adjacent to the loading dock? It must be protected from the weather. ☐ ☐ ☐

Comments: _____

_____

19. Is a dock manager's room or booth located so the manager can keep the entire dock area in view and control entrance to and exit from the building? The flow of circulation into the dock should pass this control point, and access should be restricted to authorized personnel. Security cameras may serve as a backup. ☐ ☐ ☐

Comments: _____

_____

	YES	NO	N/A

20. Are loading docks designed not to interfere with emergency egress routes from the building? ☐ ☐ ☐

   Comments: _____

21. Can examination of deliveries take place in the staging area and be monitored by the truck driver and a shipping/receiving clerk? Shipping and receiving logs should be kept. ☐ ☐ ☐

   Comments: _____

22. Is the delivery area a separate room? ☐ ☐ ☐

   Comments: _____

23. Are there two separate counters/tables in the delivery area so that delivery staff can distinguish between outgoing and incoming packages? ☐ ☐ ☐

   Comments: _____

24. Do the counters/tables have enough length and breadth to provide sufficient space for peak loading times? ☐ ☐ ☐

   Comments: _____

25. Are the counters/tables at a comfortable height so as to avoid physical injury from lifting? ☐ ☐ ☐

   Comments: _____

I. Outdoor Trash Enclosures

1. Is there provision for the temporary storage and pickup of trash? ☐ ☐ ☐

   Comments: _____

2. Is there a system in place to recycle paper, plastics, etc.? ☐ ☐ ☐

   Comments: _____

3. Are there separate containers for recyclables? ☐ ☐ ☐

   Comments: _____

4. Is the trash area secure from "dumpster divers"? ☐ ☐ ☐

   Comments: _____

	YES	NO	N/A

5. Is the trash area isolated from contact with stormwater flows originating outside the storage area? ☐ ☐ ☐

Comments: _____

_____

6. Are trash areas surrounded with a barrier sufficient to prevent all trash from being transported out of the storage area, except during collection? ☐ ☐ ☐

Comments: _____

_____

J. Outdoor Book and Media Returns

1. Is there an after-hours book and media return? ☐ ☐ ☐

Comments: _____

_____

2. Does the return have separate slots for books and media? ☐ ☐ ☐

Comments: _____

_____

3. Does the return meet ADA requirements? ☐ ☐ ☐

Comments: _____

_____

4. Is the return area well lit and secure? ☐ ☐ ☐

Comments: _____

_____

5. Is the return sheltered from the weather and small creatures? ☐ ☐ ☐

Comments: _____

_____

6. Is the return a part of the building and accessible from the inside rather than separate from the building? ☐ ☐ ☐

Comments: _____

_____

7. Is the return fire-retardant? ☐ ☐ ☐

Comments: _____

_____

8. Does the return area have a smoke detector? ☐ ☐ ☐

Comments: _____

_____

9. Is the return visible to patrons in automobiles? ☐ ☐ ☐

Comments: _____

_____

	YES	NO	N/A

10. Is the return accessible from an automobile? ☐ ☐ ☐

Comments: _____

_____

11. Is the return designed so that it will not damage library materials as it is used? ☐ ☐ ☐

Comments: _____

_____

12. Does the door on the return lock when the cart is full to prevent the cart from overflowing? ☐ ☐ ☐

Comments: _____

_____

13. Is there a locking device on outside returns? ☐ ☐ ☐

Comments: _____

_____

14. Do outside returns accommodate both walk-up and drive-up access through two deposit openings? ☐ ☐ ☐

Comments: _____

_____

Interior Organization of Library Buildings

	YES	NO	N/A

A. Entrance

1. For security purposes, is there only one public entrance/exit? ☐ ☐ ☐
   Comments: _____

2. Is the staff entrance secured from unauthorized use and well lit? ☐ ☐ ☐
   Comments: _____

3. Is the building's entrance easily identifiable to pedestrians as well as people in cars? ☐ ☐ ☐
   Comments: _____

4. Is the route from the public transportation stop to the entrance easily accessible? ☐ ☐ ☐
   Comments: _____

5. Are all building entrances sheltered from the weather and well lit? ☐ ☐ ☐
   Comments: _____

6. Is a floor covering or system provided near the entrance that allows for removal of debris from users' shoes as they walk into the building? ☐ ☐ ☐
   Comments: _____

	YES	NO	N/A

7. Is a floor drain provided for exterior rain and snow removal at the entrance
to the building?   ☐   ☐   ☐
Comments: _____
_____

8. Are there trash and cigarette receptacles near each entrance?   ☐   ☐   ☐
Comments: _____
_____

9. Are the outside telephones well lit at night and easily visible?   ☐   ☐   ☐
Comments: _____
_____

10. If the library is at an intersection, is there a main entrance at or near a corner
that will serve both streets?   ☐   ☐   ☐
Comments: _____
_____

11. Is outside seating available?   ☐   ☐   ☐
Comments: _____
_____

12. Is there a double-door vestibule to prevent drafts and heat and/or air-conditioning
losses?   ☐   ☐   ☐
Comments: _____
_____

13. Is the hardware for the entrance doors durable and sturdy enough to withstand
heavy use?   ☐   ☐   ☐
Comments: _____
_____

14. Are entrance doors easy to open and close?   ☐   ☐   ☐
Comments: _____
_____

15. Are entrance doors relatively quiet?   ☐   ☐   ☐
Comments: _____
_____

16. If glass is used near the entry, is it safety glass?   ☐   ☐   ☐
Comments: _____
_____

17. Are all public-service elements of the building easily located from the entrance? ☐   ☐   ☐
Comments: _____
_____

	YES	NO	N/A

18. Can the book security system be installed without surface-mounted wiring or carpet runners? ☐ ☐ ☐

    Comments: _____

    _____

19. If a metal studding system is used in framing the building, are wood studs used adjacent to the area where the book security system is installed to prevent interference? ☐ ☐ ☐

    Comments: _____

    _____

20. Do signs, lighting, color, and furnishings identify the various areas within the interior? ☐ ☐ ☐

    Comments: _____

    _____

21. Do the areas listed below stand out when one enters the building?

    a) Circulation ☐ ☐ ☐

    b) Reference/information ☐ ☐ ☐

    c) Catalog ☐ ☐ ☐

    d) Books/audiovisual ☐ ☐ ☐

    e) Children/adults/young adults ☐ ☐ ☐

    Comments: _____

    _____

22. Are furniture and equipment used to promote, merchandise, and display some parts of the book and media collections of the library? ☐ ☐ ☐

    Comments: _____

    _____

23. Is there space near the entrance for the following?

    a) Public bulletin boards ☐ ☐ ☐

    b) Display cases ☐ ☐ ☐

    c) Pamphlet racks ☐ ☐ ☐

    d) Announcements of library events ☐ ☐ ☐

    e) Public/community announcements bulletin boards ☐ ☐ ☐

    f) Public telephones ☐ ☐ ☐

    g) Vending machines ☐ ☐ ☐

    h) A book donation drop ☐ ☐ ☐

    i) Lobby seating ☐ ☐ ☐

    Comments: _____

    _____

24. Does there appear to be good traffic flow throughout the interior? ☐ ☐ ☐

    Comments: _____

    _____

	YES	NO	N/A

B. Circulation Desk Facilities

1. Is the circulation area located near the library's entrance?   ☐ ☐ ☐
   Comments: _____

   _____

2. Is the circulation area clearly visible and identifiable from the library's entrance?   ☐ ☐ ☐
   Comments: _____

   _____

3. Is there enough space between the circulation area and security equipment to prevent one system from interfering with the electrical and physical operation of the other?   ☐ ☐ ☐
   Comments: _____

   _____

4. Are the following functions easily identified and located by library users?
   a) Checkout   ☐ ☐ ☐
   b) Self- or express checkout (if available)   ☐ ☐ ☐
   c) Returns   ☐ ☐ ☐
   d) Issuance of new library cards   ☐ ☐ ☐
   e) Information/inquiry   ☐ ☐ ☐
   f) Reserve/holds   ☐ ☐ ☐
   g) Interlibrary loan   ☐ ☐ ☐
   h) Other functions   ☐ ☐ ☐
   Comments: _____

   _____

5. Are queuing provisions made to ensure a smooth traffic flow when entering and leaving the building without obstacles created by checkout lines during peak periods?   ☐ ☐ ☐
   Comments: _____

   _____

6. Will checkout lines be long enough to require stanchions and roping?   ☐ ☐ ☐
   Comments: _____

   _____

7. Does the circulation desk accommodate the following?
   a) Computer checkout terminals   ☐ ☐ ☐
   b) Self-checkout terminals   ☐ ☐ ☐
   c) Terminal screens that are visible to customers   ☐ ☐ ☐
   d) Telephones   ☐ ☐ ☐
   e) Answering machines   ☐ ☐ ☐

	YES	NO	N/A

f) Cash registers and/or cash drawers   ☐ ☐ ☐

g) Lost and found items   ☐ ☐ ☐

Comments: _____

_____

8. Are there sufficient sorting shelves and trucks for holding returned materials?   ☐ ☐ ☐

   Comments: _____

   _____

9. Are the shelves and trucks easily accessible and clearly arranged?   ☐ ☐ ☐

   Comments: _____

   _____

10. Can the sorting shelves accommodate all sizes of returned materials?   ☐ ☐ ☐

    Comments: _____

    _____

11. Is there an interior book drop, and can it be easily cleared?   ☐ ☐ ☐

    Comments: _____

    _____

12. Is there adequate work space for staff?   ☐ ☐ ☐

    Comments: _____

    _____

13. Are toe space and knee space incorporated into the circulation counter for staff comfort and convenience?   ☐ ☐ ☐

    Comments: _____

    _____

14. Is the circulation desk the appropriate height for adults, children, and customers with disabilities? Different heights for sections of the desk will probably be required in order to make the desk accessible and easy to use for all. Staff members may also have preferences for standing or sitting at workstations. Desks to accommodate people with disabilities also have unique requirements for knee space for people in chairs.   ☐ ☐ ☐

    Comments: _____

    _____

15. Is the desk designed for a logical workflow based on the circulation system employed by the library?   ☐ ☐ ☐

    Comments: _____

    _____

16. If there is a materials security system, is there space for the sensitizing and desensitizing equipment?   ☐ ☐ ☐

    Comments: _____

    _____

	YES	NO	N/A

17. Is there adequate space for book trucks to move about and through the circulation area? ☐ ☐ ☐

Comments: _____

_____

18. Are sorting shelves and trucks easily accessible from the return portions of the desk? ☐ ☐ ☐

Comments: _____

_____

19. Are the electrical wiring and cabling required to support equipment in the desk out of public view? ☐ ☐ ☐

Comments: _____

_____

20. Are there back panels on the computers to screen them from the public and protect against vandalism? ☐ ☐ ☐

Comments: _____

_____

21. Are the electrical wiring and cabling easily accessible by staff? ☐ ☐ ☐

Comments: _____

_____

22. Is the circulation desk designed to accommodate changing the location and size of electrical equipment in the future? This requires flexibility. ☐ ☐ ☐

Comments: _____

_____

23. Are keyboards ergonomically designed? ☐ ☐ ☐

Comments: _____

_____

24. Is the monitor screen visible to the customers? ☐ ☐ ☐

Comments: _____

_____

25. Is the top of the desk covered with a material that will not be damaged when heavy materials and equipment are dragged across or dropped on it? ☐ ☐ ☐

Comments: _____

_____

26. Is the surface of the desk smooth enough for writing? ☐ ☐ ☐

Comments: _____

_____

27. Can the desk surface be cleaned easily on a daily basis? ☐ ☐ ☐

Comments: _____

_____

	YES	NO	N/A

28. Are the height and width of the circulation desk appropriate for the various work functions taking place? ☐ ☐ ☐

Comments: _____

_____

29. Is the flooring material adjacent to the circulation counter of a type that will minimize noise of book trucks? ☐ ☐ ☐

Comments: _____

_____

30. Is the circulation desk modular in design so that modules may be interchanged as need arises? ☐ ☐ ☐

Comments: _____

_____

31. Is the desk designed to handle the necessary equipment with hidden, yet easily accessible, wiring and cable? ☐ ☐ ☐

Comments: _____

_____

32. Is there room to expand the desk as circulation of materials increases? ☐ ☐ ☐

Comments: _____

_____

33. Is there shock-absorbent flooring next to the staff side of the circulation desk? ☐ ☐ ☐

Comments: _____

_____

34. Is the floor adjacent to the circulation counter easily maintained and safe during wet weather? ☐ ☐ ☐

Comments: _____

_____

35. Are circulation staff offices located near the circulation area and easily accessible by the public? ☐ ☐ ☐

Comments: _____

_____

C. Reference Facilities

1. Is the reference desk clearly identified and conveniently located? ☐ ☐ ☐

Comments: _____

_____

		YES	NO	N/A
2.	Is the reference desk the appropriate height for adults, children, and patrons with disabilities?	☐	☐	☐

Comments: _____

_____

| 3. | Is the reference area arranged in such a manner that librarians are visibly approachable? | ☐ | ☐ | ☐ |

Comments: _____

_____

| 4. | Is the reference desk located where staff can identify by sight those customers having difficulty finding reference materials? | ☐ | ☐ | ☐ |

Comments: _____

_____

| 5. | Is there seating for customer/staff consultation? | ☐ | ☐ | ☐ |

Comments: _____

_____

| 6. | Does the library employ a "tiered" reference system? | ☐ | ☐ | ☐ |

This might include the following:

- An inquiry or informational desk at the main entrance to greet library users and direct them to the location they require
- A main reference desk employing reference specialists to answer most of the library users' questions
- Reference or bibliographic consultation stations adjacent to subject collections serviced by bibliographic specialists

Comments: _____

_____

| 7. | Can reference librarians easily get out from behind the desk to help customers? | ☐ | ☐ | ☐ |

Comments: _____

_____

| 8. | Are reference collections, including ready reference materials, conveniently located and identified? | ☐ | ☐ | ☐ |

Comments: _____

_____

| 9. | Are photocopiers close to the reference materials? | ☐ | ☐ | ☐ |

Comments: _____

_____

| 10. | Are materials and equipment requiring staff assistance grouped close to the reference service desk? | ☐ | ☐ | ☐ |

Comments: _____

_____

	YES	NO	N/A

11. Is there a terminal on the reference desk that can perform circulation functions as well as database searching functions?   ☐   ☐   ☐

Comments: _____

_____

12. Is the public access catalog accessible from all parts of the reference collection?   ☐   ☐   ☐

Comments: _____

_____

13. Are catalog terminals well distributed in the reference area?   ☐   ☐   ☐

Comments: _____

_____

14. Do reference staff members have adequate work space at their public service desk?   ☐   ☐   ☐

Comments: _____

_____

15. Does the reference desk have a cordless phone in order to allow more efficient interviews with telephoning customers while performing shelf checks?   ☐   ☐   ☐

Comments: _____

_____

16. Does the telephone system have a multiline capacity?   ☐   ☐   ☐

Comments: _____

_____

17. Are adequate space, appropriate lighting, and acoustics allowed for the following equipment and their use?

    a) Electronic workstations   ☐   ☐   ☐

    b) Audiovisual equipment   ☐   ☐   ☐

    c) Photocopiers   ☐   ☐   ☐

    d) Microform equipment   ☐   ☐   ☐

    e) Other_____   ☐   ☐   ☐

Comments: _____

_____

18. Is adequate space allowed for customer use of reference materials?   ☐   ☐   ☐

Comments: _____

_____

19. Does the reference area provide separate or acoustically isolated spaces for the following services?

    a) Interlibrary loan   ☐   ☐   ☐

    b) Database searches   ☐   ☐   ☐

    c) General information   ☐   ☐   ☐

    d) Customer interviews   ☐   ☐   ☐

    e) Telephone and/or electronic reference service   ☐   ☐   ☐

Comments: _____

_____

	YES	NO	N/A

20. If the following materials are included in the reference collection, is adequate space allowed for their use, including the staff, equipment, shelving, and furniture they require?

	YES	NO	N/A
a) General reference materials	☐	☐	☐
b) Electronic databases	☐	☐	☐
c) Newspapers	☐	☐	☐
d) Newspaper clippings	☐	☐	☐
e) Periodicals	☐	☐	☐
f) Indexes and abstracts	☐	☐	☐
g) Annual reports	☐	☐	☐
h) Microforms	☐	☐	☐
i) Rare books	☐	☐	☐
j) Bibliographies	☐	☐	☐
k) Unabridged dictionaries	☐	☐	☐
l) Government publications	☐	☐	☐
m) Vertical files	☐	☐	☐
n) College catalogs and career information	☐	☐	☐
o) Ready reference	☐	☐	☐
p) Reserves	☐	☐	☐
q) City directories	☐	☐	☐
r) Archives	☐	☐	☐
s) Telephone directories	☐	☐	☐
t) Genealogy resources	☐	☐	☐
u) Maps and atlases	☐	☐	☐
v) Audiovisual materials	☐	☐	☐
w) Tax forms	☐	☐	☐
x) General information flyers	☐	☐	☐
y) Miscellaneous library and public information	☐	☐	☐
z) Other _____	☐	☐	☐

Comments: _____

_____

21. Are reference staff offices located near the reference area?   ☐   ☐   ☐

Comments: _____

_____

22. If areas of limited or closed access exist, is adequate space allocated for

a) Staffing?	☐	☐	☐
b) Expansion?	☐	☐	☐

	YES	NO	N/A
c) Security?	☐	☐	☐

Comments: _____

23. Can the reference area be expanded for additional staff, equipment, shelving, and furniture? ☐ ☐ ☐

Comments: _____

D. Information Commons

1. Does the library have an information commons? The information commons supports and enhances student learning and research by providing state-of-the-art technology and resources in an academic environment. It is a place for students, staff, and faculty to interact, get technology support and research assistance, attend technology and research workshops or classes, and work in groups or individually on course assignments. ☐ ☐ ☐

   Comments: _____

2. Are there information and technology specialists who work side by side to serve students, faculty, and staff? ☐ ☐ ☐

   Comments: _____

3. Is there a reference and/or service desk in the information commons? ☐ ☐ ☐

   Comments: _____

4. Does the information commons offer reference services such as the following?
   a) Research for course assignments and personal interest ☐ ☐ ☐
   b) Identifying and locating library materials in all formats, including print and electronic ☐ ☐ ☐
   c) Identifying primary and secondary information sources ☐ ☐ ☐
   d) Database searching (e.g., using Boolean operators, controlled vocabulary, etc.) ☐ ☐ ☐
   e) Effective use of the Internet, including how to evaluate websites ☐ ☐ ☐

   Comments: _____

5. Are information technology courses offered by library and/or IT staff? ☐ ☐ ☐

   Comments: _____

	YES	NO	N/A

6. Does the information commons offer a variety of workstations including computers (Mac and PC), printers, scanners, and faxes? ☐ ☐ ☐

Comments: _____

_____

7. Is there a mix of individual and group workstations? ☐ ☐ ☐

Comments: _____

_____

8. Is there a replacement cycle for the hardware? ☐ ☐ ☐

Comments: _____

_____

9. Does the information commons provide access to the library's collection, the Internet, and commercial databases? ☐ ☐ ☐

Comments: _____

_____

10. Are there multimedia workstations that allow users to

    a) Digitize video from VHS, mini-DV, or camcorder? ☐ ☐ ☐

    b) Digitize analog audio from cassette tape? ☐ ☐ ☐

    c) Edit video and analog media? ☐ ☐ ☐

    d) Export digital audio and video to tape? ☐ ☐ ☐

    e) Scan images and text? ☐ ☐ ☐

    Comments: _____

    _____

11. Is there an adaptive technology center designed to assist people with disabilities? ☐ ☐ ☐

    If so, does the center include the following?

    a) High-speed scanning ☐ ☐ ☐

    b) Alternate media: braille, tactile, graphics, MP3 audiobooks, etc. ☐ ☐ ☐

    c) Hardware and software loaner programs ☐ ☐ ☐

    d) Web accessibility consulting ☐ ☐ ☐

    Comments: _____

    _____

12. Are there policies for use of the information commons, including

    a) Curtailing disruptive behavior by making people exhibiting that behavior leave? ☐ ☐ ☐

    b) Restarting computers after a specified period if a workstation is unattended and customers are waiting to use the workstation? ☐ ☐ ☐

    c) Prohibiting sleeping, offensive bodily hygiene, behavior that results in complaints or threatens to damage library property, disruptive behavior, food/beverage distribution, soliciting, roughhousing, pets, rollerblades/skates, bicycles, etc.? ☐ ☐ ☐

	YES	NO	N/A

d) Requesting that cell phones be turned off or set to "vibrate" and asking people to use phones only in areas that will not disturb other users? ☐ ☐ ☐

Comments: _____

_____

13. Does the information commons have group study rooms with computers, plasma display screens, and videotaping systems? ☐ ☐ ☐

Comments: _____

_____

E. Multimedia Facilities

1. Does the multimedia area provide an opportunity to market multimedia materials and services to users through visual and sound displays? ☐ ☐ ☐

Comments: _____

_____

2. Does the media room have a separate, independent heating/cooling system that can be regulated to control the temperature and humidity? ☐ ☐ ☐

Comments: _____

_____

3. Is there special humidifying/dehumidifying equipment to maintain a 60 percent relative humidity? ☐ ☐ ☐

Comments: _____

_____

4. Do air-conditioning units have electrostatic filters? ☐ ☐ ☐

Comments: _____

_____

5. Are supply and return air vents located high on the walls or in the ceiling with air velocities low enough to prevent draft problems with paper, hair, or clothing? ☐ ☐ ☐

Comments: _____

_____

6. Can windows be opened to provide ventilation in case the HVAC&R system breaks down? ☐ ☐ ☐

Comments: _____

_____

7. Is there sufficient acoustical treatment to prevent external noise sources from interfering with listening to media? ☐ ☐ ☐

Comments: _____

_____

	YES	NO	N/A

8. Has the following equipment been considered for placement in multimedia areas?

   a) Electronic carrels with built-in playback equipment ☐ ☐ ☐

   b) Secured and locked storage cabinets for equipment such as videotape recorders, cassette players, and overhead movie and slide projectors ☐ ☐ ☐

   c) Electronic workstations and printers ☐ ☐ ☐

   d) OPAC workstations and printers ☐ ☐ ☐

   e) Microform reader/printers ☐ ☐ ☐

   f) Podiums ☐ ☐ ☐

   g) Public-address systems ☐ ☐ ☐

   h) Tables ☐ ☐ ☐

   i) Chairs ☐ ☐ ☐

   j) Lounge furniture ☐ ☐ ☐

   k) Shelving for books and media ☐ ☐ ☐

   l) Video monitors ☐ ☐ ☐

   m) Video recorders ☐ ☐ ☐

   n) Video players ☐ ☐ ☐

   o) Projection television ☐ ☐ ☐

   p) Screen (wall or rearview) ☐ ☐ ☐

   q) Equipment that may be obsolete, but might be required to play media of interest to the library and/or its customers (such equipment might include audiocassette players, VHS machines, etc.) ☐ ☐ ☐

   Comments: _____

   _____

9. Does the facility employ an in-the-floor grid system to accommodate and easily change connections for electrical service, television, and communications distribution throughout the multimedia area? ☐ ☐ ☐

   Comments: _____

   _____

F. Media Production and Presentation Labs

1. Does the library have a media production lab? Labs may provide computers, software, and staff to assist users in the creation of multimedia-enhanced educational projects. ☐ ☐ ☐

   Comments: _____

   _____

	YES	NO	N/A

2. Does the media center have a variety of equipment available to check out to certified users? ☐ ☐ ☐

Comments: _____

_____

3. In order to check out the equipment, do users have to demonstrate competencies with the equipment and complete an equipment certification process? ☐ ☐ ☐

Comments: _____

_____

4. Does the lab staff provide training to library users? ☐ ☐ ☐

If so, does the facility have a training lab? ☐ ☐ ☐

Comments: _____

_____

5. Does the lab provide trained staff to assist customers with equipment, software, project planning, and feedback to ensure that all projects turn out as planned? ☐ ☐ ☐

Comments: _____

_____

6. Does the lab give library users access to high-end digital imaging workstations, slide and flatbed scanners, and a host of software to help digitize images and text for the Web, archiving, or any other digital presentation format? ☐ ☐ ☐

Comments: _____

_____

7. Does the lab offer a variety of tools to help assemble documents for print or digital output? ☐ ☐ ☐

Comments: _____

_____

8. Does the media lab facilitate desktop publishing by offering a variety of tools to help assemble documents for print or digital output? ☐ ☐ ☐

Comments: _____

_____

G. Special Collections/Rare Books/Archives

1. Do the building program and/or institutional guidelines spell out the security necessary in the room? ☐ ☐ ☐

Comments: _____

_____

2. Is there a desk strategically located to allow an attendant a clear view of the readers? ☐ ☐ ☐

Comments: _____

_____

	YES	NO	N/A

3. Is the reading room arranged to ensure staff observance of those who are exiting the room? ☐ ☐ ☐

Comments: _____

_____

4. Are reading tables arranged in open positions, allowing maximum supervision from staff areas? ☐ ☐ ☐

Comments: _____

_____

5. Are the reading tables generously sized individual tables with task lighting, power for typewriters and/or laptop computers, and table lecterns for holding large books? ☐ ☐ ☐

Comments: _____

_____

6. Are a few larger tables provided for use of large folios? ☐ ☐ ☐

Comments: _____

_____

7. Are the rare books housed in locked cases with grilled doors? ☐ ☐ ☐

Comments: _____

_____

8. Are the rare books shelved in specially designed (padded) book stacks that are securely braced with earthquake safety devices to prevent books from falling off shelves? ☐ ☐ ☐

Comments: _____

_____

9. Are manuscripts and archives housed in acid-free boxes? ☐ ☐ ☐

Comments: _____

_____

10. Are microfilm reading machines and other equipment provided to "read" all the types of media and materials located in the room? ☐ ☐ ☐

Comments: _____

_____

11. Are reading and exhibit areas separated? ☐ ☐ ☐

Comments: _____

_____

12. Can an even temperature of 70 degrees Fahrenheit and humidity of about 50 percent be maintained to prolong the life of the books and materials? ☐ ☐ ☐

Comments: _____

_____

	YES	NO	N/A

13. Is there an electrostatic filter for the removal of dust and dirt? ☐ ☐ ☐

    Comments: _____

    _____

14. Is there a backup mechanical filter should the electrostatic filter break down? ☐ ☐ ☐

    Comments: _____

    _____

15. Is the location of the air intake high enough on the exterior wall or roof to avoid chemical and exhaust pollution, especially for libraries sited in urban areas? ☐ ☐ ☐

    Comments: _____

    _____

16. Is care taken to control the levels of damaging (especially ultraviolet) light? ☐ ☐ ☐

    Comments: _____

    _____

17. Is the area monitored for insects, rodents, and other biological pests that may attack the collection? (Mechanical and/or chemical control techniques can be used.) ☐ ☐ ☐

    Comments: _____

    _____

18. Is the area monitored and protected to provide security with the following?

    a) A vault or strong room ☐ ☐ ☐

    b) Special restricted keying and access ☐ ☐ ☐

    c) Intrusion alarms ☐ ☐ ☐

    d) Door contacts and other forms of perimeter protection ☐ ☐ ☐

    e) Smoke and fire alarms ☐ ☐ ☐

    f) Monitoring controls and alarms to indicate changes from desired temperature and/or humidity ☐ ☐ ☐

    g) Water alarms ☐ ☐ ☐

    h) Special alarms in display cases ☐ ☐ ☐

    i) Panic alarms for staff ☐ ☐ ☐

    j) Security video cameras to monitor the collection and reading areas ☐ ☐ ☐

    Comments: _____

    _____

19. Has the library instituted a policy for responding to alarms and specifying where their signals should be seen or heard? ☐ ☐ ☐

    Comments: _____

    _____

20. Is adequate work space provided for conservation work? ☐ ☐ ☐

    Comments: _____

    _____

	YES	NO	N/A

21. Is a disaster preparedness plan in effect?   ☐   ☐   ☐

Comments: _____

_____

H. Reserve Book Room

1. Does the library have a reserve book room? The reserve book room provides
access to course-related books that faculty members have placed in the library for
their students to borrow for short periods.   ☐   ☐   ☐

Comments: _____

_____

2. What is kept in the reserve book room?

   a) Items selected by instructors that are needed by students for class assignments   ☐   ☐   ☐

   b) High-demand items selected by the university library to allocate use   ☐   ☐   ☐

Comments: _____

_____

3. Can the materials in the reserve book room be checked out?   ☐   ☐   ☐

   a) If yes, for how long may the materials be checked out? _____

   _____

   b) Are there multiple loan periods?   ☐   ☐   ☐

Comments: _____

_____

4. Are electronic reserves available on workstations in the room? An electronic
reserve system is a web-based system for articles, course notes, and other
supplemental materials. The library usually takes care of scanning, document
management, and copyright permissions.   ☐   ☐   ☐

Comments: _____

_____

5. Are the paper reserves kept in closed stacks accessible only by the staff?   ☐   ☐   ☐

   If not, are they on open shelves in the reserve book area?   ☐   ☐   ☐

Comments: _____

_____

6. Is the reserve book room open for different periods than the main library?   ☐   ☐   ☐

   If so, how is access obtained to the rare book room when the main library is closed? _____

   _____

Comments: _____

_____

7. Is there duplication equipment in the reserve book room for copying documents
and books?   ☐   ☐   ☐

Comments: _____

_____

	YES	NO	N/A

I.   Faculty/Graduate Carrels and Study Rooms

1. Are there library carrels and small study rooms that may be reserved for extended periods by faculty and graduate students?   ☐ ☐ ☐
    Comments: _____
    _____

2. Has a means of allocating study rooms and carrels been established?   ☐ ☐ ☐
    Comments: _____
    _____

3. How long may the study rooms and carrels be reserved, and how may they be renewed? _____
    _____
    Comments: _____
    _____

4. Are there key locks on the assigned carrels and study rooms?   ☐ ☐ ☐
    Comments: _____
    _____

5. If there are key locks, who controls the issuance of the keys? _____
    _____
    Comments: _____
    _____

6. Do books used in the carrels and study rooms have to be checked out if they are kept in the carrels and study rooms?   ☐ ☐ ☐
    Comments: _____
    _____

J.   Literacy Center

1. Does the library provide literacy or reading center service?   ☐ ☐ ☐
    Comments: _____
    _____

2. Is the literacy center a separate room or area in the library?   ☐ ☐ ☐
    Comments: _____
    _____

3. Is there office space and equipment for the literacy program manager?   ☐ ☐ ☐
    Comments: _____
    _____

4. Is space provided for a public bulletin/display board and brochure rack?   ☐ ☐ ☐
    Comments: _____
    _____

	YES	NO	N/A

5. Is there space for a literacy book collection? ☐ ☐ ☐

Comments: _____

6. Are there two-position tutoring study carrels for learner and tutor interaction? ☐ ☐ ☐

Comments: _____

7. Is there space for computer learning stations? (Each station should have seating for two [learner and tutor], a computer with appropriate software, and storage for software and supplies.) ☐ ☐ ☐

Comments: _____

8. Is the lab acoustically controlled so that noise will not impact learners using the lab or other areas of the learning center? ☐ ☐ ☐

Comments: _____

9. Is there a small conference room that might serve as a functional office as well as a place for informal discussion? ☐ ☐ ☐

Comments: _____

10. Are there workstations or work areas for staff? ☐ ☐ ☐

Comments: _____

11. Are there workstations or work areas for volunteers? ☐ ☐ ☐

Comments: _____

K. Young Adult Facilities

1. Did a teen advisory panel work with the design team in developing the young adult space? ☐ ☐ ☐

Comments: _____

2. Is the location of the young adult area easily determined when one enters the library? ☐ ☐ ☐

Comments: _____

3. Is the young adult section separate from other areas in the library? ☐ ☐ ☐

Comments: _____

		YES	NO	N/A

4. Is the space closer to the adult section than to the children's section?   ☐ ☐ ☐

    Comments: _____

    _____

5. Does the space encourage young adult use by allowing them to "control" it as they control personal space in their homes?   ☐ ☐ ☐

    Comments: _____

    _____

6. Is the space slightly secluded, giving the appearance of privacy, while still allowing some supervision?   ☐ ☐ ☐

    Comments: _____

    _____

7. Does the space include glassed-in and acoustically separate seminar rooms that allow group study?   ☐ ☐ ☐

    Comments: _____

    _____

8. Does the space include a glassed-in and acoustically separate area with a large-screen television and audio equipment?   ☐ ☐ ☐

    Comments: _____

    _____

9. Do the materials housed in the young adult area appeal to the intended audience?   ☐ ☐ ☐

    Comments: _____

    _____

10. Are materials such as paperbacks in multiple copies arranged as in bookstores, the shelves uncluttered, and collections grouped by genre such as science fiction, romance, and mystery?   ☐ ☐ ☐

    Comments: _____

    _____

11. Are the shelving and fixtures used to store young adult materials similar to those found in music, video, and book stores?   ☐ ☐ ☐

    Comments: _____

    _____

12. Does the space include computers for word processing and spreadsheets, access to the Internet, and games?   ☐ ☐ ☐

    Comments: _____

    _____

13. Is there secure and adequate space to store teen gear such as skateboards and backpacks?   ☐ ☐ ☐

    Comments: _____

    _____

	YES	NO	N/A

14. Does the space allow a variety of comfortable seating options including traditional seating, chairs designed to tilt back without tipping, couches, and floor seating? ☐ ☐ ☐

Comments: _____

_____

15. Is there space allocated to reflect young adult pride and activities including bulletin boards listing teen accomplishments and activities? ☐ ☐ ☐

Comments: _____

_____

L. Children's Facilities

1. Is the physical and psychological environment pleasant and inviting to children? If you were a child, would this area appeal to you? ☐ ☐ ☐

Comments: _____

_____

2. Is the children's area arranged in such a manner that adults are not reluctant to use it? ☐ ☐ ☐

Comments: _____

_____

3. If there is a children's staff office, is it of adequate size? ☐ ☐ ☐

Comments: _____

_____

4. Is there a separate children's card catalog or an online public access terminal? ☐ ☐ ☐

Comments: _____

_____

5. Are shelving and furniture scaled for children? ☐ ☐ ☐

Comments: _____

_____

6. Are there small alcoves, surrounded by low shelves, controllable by the staff but accessible to children, where the children may pick out a book or game and settle individually or in small groups to enjoy it? ☐ ☐ ☐

Comments: _____

_____

7. Are the drinking fountains scaled for children? ☐ ☐ ☐

Comments: _____

_____

8. Are there restrooms scaled for children in the children's area? ☐ ☐ ☐

Comments: _____

_____

	YES	NO	N/A

9. Does one or more of the children's restrooms include a diaper-changing table? ☐ ☐ ☐
    Comments: _____
    _____

10. If restroom facilities are not located in the children's area, are they located adjacent to or near the children's area? ☐ ☐ ☐
    Comments: _____
    _____

11. Are there some imaginative pieces of furniture for visual surprise? ☐ ☐ ☐
    Comments: _____
    _____

12. Are cheerful colors, interesting geometric shapes, and graphic sketches used in the children's area? ☐ ☐ ☐
    Comments: _____
    _____

13. Have sharp corners and edges been eliminated from furniture and equipment? ☐ ☐ ☐
    Comments: _____
    _____

14. Are the tabletops, chairs, and floors easily cleaned? ☐ ☐ ☐
    Comments: _____
    _____

15. Is there comfortable adult seating for use while adults are sharing books with children? ☐ ☐ ☐
    Comments: _____
    _____

16. Does the staff have visual control of the area? ☐ ☐ ☐
    Comments: _____
    _____

17. Is realia conveniently and attractively housed? ☐ ☐ ☐
    Comments: _____
    _____

18. Is there sufficient space for use and secure storage (locked, if needed) of audiovisual materials and equipment? ☐ ☐ ☐
    Comments: _____
    _____

19. Is there sufficient space for crafts activities and storage of crafts materials? ☐ ☐ ☐
    Comments: _____
    _____

	YES	NO	N/A

20. Is the floor a single height to allow for flexibility in programming and accessibility, as well as to avoid injuries? ☐ ☐ ☐

Comments: _____

21. Is there a separate programming area adjacent to the children's area but out of the traffic flow? ☐ ☐ ☐

Comments: _____

22. Is the programming area designed to be multipurpose when not used for special functions, that is, quiet study, computer resource center, etc.? ☐ ☐ ☐

Comments: _____

23. Is the programming area designed to handle the full age range of children who use the library? ☐ ☐ ☐

Comments: _____

24. Has allowance been made for storage of special equipment used in programming, such as a puppet stage? ☐ ☐ ☐

Comments: _____

25. Is the children's area acoustically designed to avoid interfering with other library functions? ☐ ☐ ☐

Comments: _____

26. Do interior finishes and materials enhance the acoustics? ☐ ☐ ☐

Comments: _____

27. Are play areas designed to avoid interfering with other library functions? ☐ ☐ ☐

Comments: _____

28. Has allowance been made for specific displays and materials geared to children? ☐ ☐ ☐

Comments: _____

29. If children's and adult circulation counters are not separated, is there lower counter space set aside for children, visibly marked by large graphics? ☐ ☐ ☐

Comments: _____

	YES	NO	N/A

30. Has sufficient space been allowed for easy access by children if materials are checked out or returned at the children's desk?   ☐ ☐ ☐

   Comments: _____

   _____

M. Meeting and Seminar Rooms

1. Is the meeting-room entry close to the main entrance?   ☐ ☐ ☐

   Comments: _____

   _____

2. Is there an assembly area adequate in size for handling the arrival and departure of large groups that may be attending meetings?   ☐ ☐ ☐

   Comments: _____

   _____

3. Can the meeting-room area be closed off from the remainder of the library?   ☐ ☐ ☐

   Comments: _____

   _____

4. When the meeting room is closed off from the rest of the library, do users have access to public restrooms?   ☐ ☐ ☐

   Comments: _____

   _____

5. Are floor coverings easy to clean and replace?   ☐ ☐ ☐

   Comments: _____

   _____

6. Is a portable or built-in stage required?   ☐ ☐ ☐

   Comments: _____

   _____

7. Will a lectern or podium be required?   ☐ ☐ ☐

   Comments: _____

   _____

8. Is there a public telephone that may be used when the library is closed?   ☐ ☐ ☐

   Comments: _____

   _____

9. Is there a drinking fountain that may be used when the library is closed?   ☐ ☐ ☐

   Comments: _____

   _____

	YES	NO	N/A

10. If the meeting room is large, is it equipped with folding doors that can be used as dividers to split the room into two or more parts? ☐ ☐ ☐

Comments: _____

_____

11. If folding partitions are used, can users get to and from each meeting room without disturbing those in adjacent rooms? ☐ ☐ ☐

Comments: _____

_____

12. Are there provisions for hanging coats and other personal gear? ☐ ☐ ☐

Comments: _____

_____

13. Does the room provide flexibility to accommodate a variety of programming activities, from children's story hours to film showings to art exhibitions? ☐ ☐ ☐

Comments: _____

_____

14. Are there special lighting fixtures located in the ceiling above the speaker and controlled by dimmer switches to provide glare-free and appropriate lighting? ☐ ☐ ☐

Comments: _____

_____

15. Is the lighting controllable in intensity, allowing full darkening of the room for visual presentations? ☐ ☐ ☐

Comments: _____

_____

16. Are window coverings provided to darken the room and block out light for visual presentations? ☐ ☐ ☐

Comments: _____

_____

17. Is there a kitchenette for the preparation of food and for serving light refreshments? ☐ ☐ ☐

Comments: _____

_____

18. Are there provisions for a lockable pass-through from the kitchen to the meeting room for food and beverage service? ☐ ☐ ☐

Comments: _____

_____

19. Is the kitchen equipped with a sink, garbage disposal, microwave oven, stove, refrigerator, icemaker, and cabinets for storage of dishes and equipment? ☐ ☐ ☐

Comments: _____

_____

	YES	NO	N/A

20. Is the room appropriately wired for phone, cable, teleconferencing, etc.? ☐ ☐ ☐
Comments: _____
_____

21. Are there electrical and telecommunications outlets on all walls and at needed locations on the floor? ☐ ☐ ☐
Comments: _____
_____

22. Are adequate space, data lines, and power provided for the following equipment?
    a) Overhead projectors ☐ ☐ ☐
    b) Projection from portable and built-in computers ☐ ☐ ☐
    c) 35 mm slide projectors ☐ ☐ ☐
    d) Ceiling- or wall-mounted screens ☐ ☐ ☐
    e) Large-screen or projection televisions ☐ ☐ ☐
    f) Video recorders and players ☐ ☐ ☐
    g) Teleconferencing equipment ☐ ☐ ☐
    h) Audio sound system using radio, MP3 players, and compact discs ☐ ☐ ☐
    i) Public-address system ☐ ☐ ☐
    j) Wireless microphones ☐ ☐ ☐
    k) Podium with links to the various sound systems ☐ ☐ ☐
    l) Cable and/or satellite-dish equipment ☐ ☐ ☐
Comments: _____
_____

23. Is there lockable storage for equipment? ☐ ☐ ☐
Comments: _____
_____

24. Are there blackboards and/or white marker boards? ☐ ☐ ☐
Comments: _____
_____

25. Are there electronic boards? ☐ ☐ ☐
Comments: _____
_____

26. Are there art rails for exhibitions? ☐ ☐ ☐
Comments: _____
_____

27. Are caddies available to move and store the chairs? ☐ ☐ ☐
Comments: _____
_____

	YES	NO	N/A
28. Are the tables folding?	☐	☐	☐
Comments: _____
_____
29. Does the folding mechanism of the tables operate easily?	☐	☐	☐
Comments: _____
_____
30. Do the tables have			
a) Fixed-height bases?	☐	☐	☐
b) Adjustable-height bases?	☐	☐	☐
Comments: _____
_____
31. Are caddies available to store and move the tables?	☐	☐	☐
Comments: _____
_____
32. Are the chairs and tables light enough to be moved and maneuvered by library staff?	☐	☐	☐
Comments: _____
_____
33. Are there lockable storage areas near meeting rooms for audiovisual equipment and/or furniture such as lecterns or stackable chairs?	☐	☐	☐
Comments: _____
_____
34. Have provisions been made to prevent noisy programs from interfering with library operations?	☐	☐	☐
Comments: _____
_____

N. Convenience Facilities

	YES	NO	N/A
1. Are restrooms located close to the lobby or building entrance?	☐	☐	☐
Comments: _____
_____
2. Does every floor have restrooms for both men and women?	☐	☐	☐
Comments: _____
_____
3. Are restrooms easily identified?	☐	☐	☐
Comments: _____
_____

		YES	NO	N/A
4.	Are there special restrooms for children, located in or near the children's area?	☐	☐	☐
	Comments: _____			
5.	Do all restrooms contain an area for changing children's diapers?	☐	☐	☐
	Comments: _____			
6.	Does every floor have a drinking fountain?	☐	☐	☐
	Comments: _____			
7.	Are there drinking fountains for children?	☐	☐	☐
	Comments: _____			
8.	Are public telephones available?	☐	☐	☐
	Comments: _____			
9.	Are telephones strategically located to encourage convenient use while preventing disturbance to other customers?	☐	☐	☐
	Comments: _____			
10.	Are telephone directories provided?	☐	☐	☐
	Comments: _____			
11.	Is space allocated for public access to the following?			
	a) Photocopiers	☐	☐	☐
	b) Telefacsimile (fax) machines	☐	☐	☐
	c) Personal computers	☐	☐	☐
	d) Computer printers	☐	☐	☐
	e) Audiovisual equipment	☐	☐	☐
	f) Other _____	☐	☐	☐
	Comments: _____			
12.	Are signs available identifying these machines?	☐	☐	☐
	Comments: _____			
13.	Are coin-changing machines located near these machines?	☐	☐	☐
	Comments: _____			

	YES	NO	N/A
14. Are provisions made for noise abatement in noisy areas of the library?	☐	☐	☐
Comments: _____			
15. Are provisions made for trash and recycling?	☐	☐	☐
Comments: _____			
16. Is there a refreshment area available for the public?	☐	☐	☐
Comments: _____			
17. Are vending machines available for public use?	☐	☐	☐
Comments: _____			
18. Is the refreshment area located away from public service areas?	☐	☐	☐
Comments: _____			
19. Is the refreshment area easily viewed and supervised by staff?	☐	☐	☐
Comments: _____			
20. Are trash receptacles available?	☐	☐	☐
Comments: _____			
21. Are clocks strategically located and visible in every major public area?	☐	☐	☐
Comments: _____			
22. Are the clocks controlled electronically to centrally adjust if needed?	☐	☐	☐
If not, are they easily accessible for resetting the time?	☐	☐	☐
Comments: _____			
23. If smoking is permitted, are smoking areas clearly identified?	☐	☐	☐
Comments: _____			
24. Is there a separate elevator for staff?	☐	☐	☐
Comments: _____			
25. Is there a separate elevator for freight?	☐	☐	☐
Comments: _____			

	YES	NO	N/A

O. Displays

1. Are the display furnishings and shelving appropriate for merchandising the library's products and services?   ☐ ☐ ☐
   Comments: _____
   _____

2. Can library materials be arranged in an attractive, appealing way to promote library products?   ☐ ☐ ☐
   Comments: _____
   _____

3. Does the display shelving have built-in signs, boards, and lights to draw the attention of the library user?   ☐ ☐ ☐
   Comments: _____
   _____

4. Are the racks for displaying audiovisual materials stable when filled?   ☐ ☐ ☐
   Comments: _____
   _____

5. Are there bulletin boards for community notices and activities?   ☐ ☐ ☐
   Comments: _____
   _____

6. Are there secure and locked exhibit cases, both freestanding and built-in?   ☐ ☐ ☐
   Comments: _____
   _____

7. Do the cases have nonglare lighting to highlight the exhibits?   ☐ ☐ ☐
   Comments: _____
   _____

8. Do the cases have surfaces that make posting easy?   ☐ ☐ ☐
   Comments: _____
   _____

9. Are the cases ventilated to avoid overheating and damaging the exhibits?   ☐ ☐ ☐
   Comments: _____
   _____

10. Are display cases located in high-traffic areas to make these areas more visually interesting?   ☐ ☐ ☐
    Comments: _____
    _____

11. Is there space for the distribution of community information, tax forms, flyers, and other handouts?   ☐ ☐ ☐
    Comments: _____
    _____

	YES	NO	N/A

12. Is there a clear modular system of racks and displays for distribution of community notices and/or giveaway items to prevent clutter?   ☐   ☐   ☐

Comments: _____

_____

13. Are the racks and displays for distributing materials flexible enough to handle a variety of sizes and shapes of literature in a neat, attractive manner?   ☐   ☐   ☐

Comments: _____

_____

14. Are the racks displayed in highly visible locations in order to attract customers and merchandise materials?   ☐   ☐   ☐

Comments: _____

_____

P.   Public Art

1. Will public art be integrated into the new library or library expansion/ renovation? Public art refers to works of art in any media that have been planned and executed with the specific intention of being sited or staged in or around the library. It is usually permanent or long-term art, and not a temporary exhibit.   ☐   ☐   ☐

Comments: _____

_____

2. Does the library have a policy covering gifts of art from a donor?   ☐   ☐   ☐

Comments: _____

_____

3. In a building construction project, is a percentage of the construction budget set aside for artwork?   ☐   ☐   ☐

Comments: _____

_____

4. In a construction project, how are artists selected?

   a) By direct election, whereby the artist is selected directly by the library or a committee from the university, political jurisdiction, board, etc.   ☐   ☐   ☐

   b) By limited competition, whereby the artist is invited by the library, university, political jurisdiction, board, etc. to submit proposals   ☐   ☐   ☐

   c) By open competition, whereby any artist or design team applies in response to a request for proposal/qualification and is selected by the library, university, political jurisdiction, board, etc.   ☐   ☐   ☐

   d) By the architect, for whom the artist is a subconsultant   ☐   ☐   ☐

   Comments: _____

   _____

	YES	NO	N/A

5.   If the library issues a request for proposal (RFP) from artists:

   a) Is the RFP advertised in local newspapers, in newsletters, by direct mail, or by other approved methods? ☐ ☐ ☐

   b) Is a committee in place to screen responses to the RFP? ☐ ☐ ☐

   c) Who is responsible for the ultimate selection of the artist? _____
   _____

   Comments: _____
   _____

6.   In choosing the artist and the artist's work, consider the following factors in the selection process.

   a) *Completeness of response to the RFP.* Does the artist address each issue as set forth in the RFP? ☐ ☐ ☐

   b) *Quality.* Is the highest priority given to the artist with the best quality artwork? ☐ ☐ ☐

   c) *Medium.* Are all types of media considered for public art? ☐ ☐ ☐

   d) *Style.* Are all styles of art considered? ☐ ☐ ☐

   e) *Nature.* Is the art appropriate in scale, material, form, and content for the physical space being considered for the art? ☐ ☐ ☐

   f) *Permanence.* In addition to the quality of the art, will the art be relatively permanent, protected against theft and vandalism, and easy to maintain, and will it stand up well to ambient conditions? ☐ ☐ ☐

   g) *Ability to add to the architectural project.* Will the art enhance the architecture of the new library or the library expansion? ☐ ☐ ☐

   h) *Construction.* Is the art engineered for safety and technical feasibility? ☐ ☐ ☐

   i) *Standards.* Does the art meet the standards and policies of the library? ☐ ☐ ☐

   Comments: _____
   _____

7.   Does the artist's involvement in the construction project include the following?

   a) Being involved at the inception of the project so that the art is integral to the design ☐ ☐ ☐

   b) Having his or her concepts included when the overall design of the project is first presented to the client and the community ☐ ☐ ☐

   c) Having his or her ideas incorporated into the construction documents and bid as an integral part of the construction project ☐ ☐ ☐

   d) Subcontracting directly with the lead architect or engineer ☐ ☐ ☐

   e) Receiving a fee for design and negotiating fees for oversight of fabrication and installation on an as needed basis ☐ ☐ ☐

   Comments: _____
   _____

	YES	NO	N/A

8. Is there a policy in place to govern the decommissioning and disposal of the art? ☐ ☐ ☐

   Comments: _____

   _____

Q. Interior Signage

1. Do signs meet ADA requirements (see chapter 6 of this book)? ☐ ☐ ☐

   Comments: _____

   _____

2. Has the sign system been integrated into the building design and furniture selection process (architecture, color, etc.)? ☐ ☐ ☐

   Comments: _____

   _____

3. Is there consistency in signage throughout the building? Signs that serve the same function throughout the building should have the same shape, size, layout, type size, and placement. ☐ ☐ ☐

   Comments: _____

   _____

4. Are the signs of good design? Typeface, size, spacing of letters, contrast, use of symbols, and color should all be considered. ☐ ☐ ☐

   Comments: _____

   _____

5. Are the sizes of signs proportional to distance from users? ☐ ☐ ☐

   Comments: _____

   _____

6. Are signs sequentially positioned to facilitate self-service? ☐ ☐ ☐

   Comments: _____

   _____

7. Are the signs well lit, easy to read, and positioned for a clear view? ☐ ☐ ☐

   Comments: _____

   _____

8. Do signs use terminology consistently? Only one term should be applied to any one area, service, etc. ☐ ☐ ☐

   Comments: _____

   _____

9. Is the text of the sign clearly and accurately written in order to communicate the intended message effectively and positively? ☐ ☐ ☐

   Comments: _____

   _____

	YES	NO	N/A

10. Is the signage system flexible enough that, as conditions change, signs can be changed or moved easily?

☐ ☐ ☐

Comments: _____

_____

11. Is redundancy avoided? Too many signs, all providing the same message, can be as bad as no sign at all.

☐ ☐ ☐

Comments: _____

_____

12. Are signs positioned and designed to avoid injuries (no sharp corners, sufficient height, etc.)?

☐ ☐ ☐

Comments: _____

_____

13. Are signs reasonably vandal proof?

☐ ☐ ☐

Comments: _____

_____

14. Is the exterior monument sign(s) identifying the library positioned so that it is easy to read when approaching the library? A sign perpendicular to the road is easier to read than a sign parallel to the road.

☐ ☐ ☐

Comments: _____

_____

15. Is there a directory identifying major library services and their locations?

☐ ☐ ☐

Comments: _____

_____

16. Are directional signs available leading customers to different departments and placed at logical decision points?

☐ ☐ ☐

Comments: _____

_____

17. Are there signs on doors and at the entrances to departments to identify the function or service within that room or area?

☐ ☐ ☐

Comments: _____

_____

18. Are there signs to highlight temporary collections and services or to announce events taking place in the library?

☐ ☐ ☐

Comments: _____

_____

19. Are there signs that can be easily changed on the end panels of stacks to identify which books are shelved in that range?

☐ ☐ ☐

Comments: _____

_____

	YES	NO	N/A

20. Are there signs to provide critical information about regulations, warnings, procedures, instructions, and hours? ☐ ☐ ☐

Comments: _____

_____

21. Are instructional signs available for use at electronic workstations? ☐ ☐ ☐

Comments: _____

_____

R. Workrooms/Offices

1. Are there individual workstations for all staff? ☐ ☐ ☐

Comments: _____

_____

2. Are there adequate workstations for library volunteers? ☐ ☐ ☐

Comments: _____

_____

3. Are workstations free from distractions? ☐ ☐ ☐

Comments: _____

_____

4. When required for team activities, are some workstations designed to foster communication among staff? ☐ ☐ ☐

Comments: _____

_____

5. Are there lockers and/or coat closets where personal items can be stored and secured for staff and volunteers? ☐ ☐ ☐

Comments: _____

_____

6. Is there adequate at-hand storage space? ☐ ☐ ☐

Comments: _____

_____

7. Is there a sickbay area or a place where ill staff members may rest? ☐ ☐ ☐

Comments: _____

_____

8. Is there adequate space for equipment such as electronic workstations and television/DVD units? ☐ ☐ ☐

Comments: _____

_____

		YES	NO	N/A

9.   Is there adequate space for a variety of types of library storage?   ☐ ☐ ☐

Comments: _____

_____

10. Is there a locking storage unit or area to secure valuable equipment such as CD and DVD players, video projectors, and cameras?   ☐ ☐ ☐

Comments: _____

_____

11. Is there a locking storage unit to secure media and other expensive items during processing and prior to delivery to the public shelves?   ☐ ☐ ☐

Comments: _____

_____

12. Is there adequate space for technical services operations?   ☐ ☐ ☐

Comments: _____

_____

13. Are there adequate sorting shelves for the storage of returned library items?   ☐ ☐ ☐

Comments: _____

_____

14. Is there an electronic workstation(s) with a printer(s) in the workroom to check in library items and look up records?   ☐ ☐ ☐

Comments: _____

_____

15. Is there a typewriter in addition to the electronic workstation?   ☐ ☐ ☐

Comments: _____

_____

16. Are there telephones?   ☐ ☐ ☐

Comments: _____

_____

17. Are there enough electrical outlets for all required equipment?   ☐ ☐ ☐

Comments: _____

_____

18. Are there enough data lines?   ☐ ☐ ☐

Comments: _____

_____

19. Is there adequate space for book trucks at workstations and for their storage when not in use?   ☐ ☐ ☐

Comments: _____

_____

	YES	NO	N/A

20. Are the workflow pattern and room arrangement effective and conducive to staff productivity? ☐ ☐ ☐

Comments: _____

_____

21. Are environmental conditions such as lighting, HVAC&R, and acoustics adequate and comfortable? ☐ ☐ ☐

Comments: _____

_____

22. Are managers' offices separate, in enclosed rooms, to ensure privacy? ☐ ☐ ☐

Comments: _____

_____

23. Are there electronic workstations in the managers' offices for typing evaluations and other confidential types of materials? ☐ ☐ ☐

Comments: _____

_____

24. Does the public have convenient access to the offices of those managers who interact with the public? ☐ ☐ ☐

Comments: _____

_____

25. Does the manager have convenient access to the workroom from his or her office? ☐ ☐ ☐

Comments: _____

_____

26. Are there provisions for U.S. mail and newspaper delivery when the library is closed? ☐ ☐ ☐

Comments: _____

_____

S. Staff Lounge

1. Are there lockers and/or coat closets where personal items can be stored and secured for staff and volunteers? ☐ ☐ ☐

Comments: _____

_____

2. Is there a kitchen for the preparation of food and for serving light refreshments? ☐ ☐ ☐

Comments: _____

_____

3. Is the kitchen equipped with a sink, garbage disposal, microwave oven, stove, refrigerator, icemaker, coffee maker, and cabinets for storage of dishes and equipment? ☐ ☐ ☐

Comments: _____

_____

		YES	NO	N/A

4. Is there provision for a ventilating system to eliminate strong food odors?   ☐ ☐ ☐

 Comments: _____

_____

5. Are there vending machines for food and soft drinks?   ☐ ☐ ☐

 Comments: _____

_____

6. Are there adequate numbers of tables and chairs to accommodate all staff that may be using the lounge at the same time?   ☐ ☐ ☐

 Comments: _____

_____

7. Is there a cot/sofa that can be used by the staff or customers in case of an emergency?   ☐ ☐ ☐

 Comments: _____

_____

8. Is there a window to look out on a quiet, pleasant scene?   ☐ ☐ ☐

 Comments: _____

_____

9. Does the staff have restrooms separate from those for the public?   ☐ ☐ ☐

 Comments: _____

_____

10. Is the staff lounge acoustically treated to eliminate the transfer of sound to and from adjacent public and staff areas?   ☐ ☐ ☐

 Comments: _____

_____

T. Friends of the Library

1. Does the library have a Friends of the Library group?   ☐ ☐ ☐

 Comments: _____

_____

2. Do the Friends of the Library accept donations such as books (used/new) and other items (puzzles, magazines, audiovisual)?   ☐ ☐ ☐

 Comments: _____

_____

3. Do the Friends of the Library have their own counter or worktable to sort donated items?   ☐ ☐ ☐

 Comments: _____

_____

	YES	NO	N/A

4. Do the Friends of the Library have equipment such as carts and dollies available to handle large donations of books and media?   ☐ ☐ ☐

   Comments: _____

5. Do the Friends of the Library have convenient storage for the above equipment and cardboard boxes for packing the donated items?   ☐ ☐ ☐

   Comments: _____

6. Are the donations placed on shelves on the premises so the staff can view and select whatever they want to add to their collection, send to the branch book exchange, or sell?   ☐ ☐ ☐

   Comments: _____

7. Is there storage space either on or off the premises for the donated items?   ☐ ☐ ☐

   Comments: _____

8. Do the Friends of the Library operate a retail store?   ☐ ☐ ☐

   Comments: _____

9. Do the Friends have an
   a) Annual book sale?   ☐ ☐ ☐
   b) Ongoing daily book sale?   ☐ ☐ ☐

   Comments: _____

10. If the Friends have an ongoing daily sale, do they sell their items from
    a) A store?   ☐ ☐ ☐
    b) Some shelves in the library?   ☐ ☐ ☐
    c) A book cart?   ☐ ☐ ☐
    d) An area adjacent to their room?   ☐ ☐ ☐

    Comments: _____

11. Is the book sale area clearly marked by signs?   ☐ ☐ ☐

    Comments: _____

12. Is the cash from the Friends' sales kept in a separate place so as not to get confused with the daily cash from library transactions?   ☐ ☐ ☐

    Comments: _____

	YES	NO	N/A

13. Is there space in a prominent area allotted to the Friends for their newsletter and membership applications? ☐ ☐ ☐

Comments: _____

_____

14. Do the Friends have a mail slot to receive their membership applications, dues, donations, etc.? ☐ ☐ ☐

Comments: _____

_____

15. Do the Friends have a bulletin board for messages? ☐ ☐ ☐

Comments: _____

_____

16. Do the Friends have some space in the staff lounge to hang their coats, and lockers or some other safe place to store their valuables? ☐ ☐ ☐

Comments: _____

_____

U. Library Store

1. If a library store is provided, is the store in a prominent location to attract the attention of customers as they walk by? ☐ ☐ ☐

Comments: _____

_____

2. Are there adequate signage, window displays, and other visual cues to market the library store to potential customers? ☐ ☐ ☐

Comments: _____

_____

3. Are the circulation paths simple and logical? Customers should be able to concentrate on the merchandise and not be worried about bumping into things. ☐ ☐ ☐

Comments: _____

_____

4. Is the cash/wrapping counter designed and located for maximum efficiency, accessibility, and optimal equipment placement? ☐ ☐ ☐

Comments: _____

_____

5. Is there a cash register? ☐ ☐ ☐

Comments: _____

_____

		YES	NO	N/A
6.	Is there an office/storage room located in the store?	☐	☐	☐

Comments: _____

_____

| 7. | Is the design of the display fixtures flexible to permit new products to be added periodically? | ☐ | ☐ | ☐ |

Comments: _____

_____

| 8. | Will some products require special displays or display techniques? | ☐ | ☐ | ☐ |

Comments: _____

_____

| 9. | Is a specific lighting source (incandescent, fluorescent, or halogen) preferred? | ☐ | ☐ | ☐ |

Comments: _____

_____

| 10. | Are there security systems in place to protect staff, merchandise, and cash? | ☐ | ☐ | ☐ |

Comments: _____

_____

| 11. | Are there special requirements for cooling or heating any areas of the store? | ☐ | ☐ | ☐ |

Comments: _____

_____

| 12. | Are telephone and data connections required? | ☐ | ☐ | ☐ |

Comments: _____

_____

| 13. | Are there enough electrical outlets? | ☐ | ☐ | ☐ |

Comments: _____

_____

| 14. | Will the store have a sound system? | ☐ | ☐ | ☐ |

Comments: _____

_____

| 15. | Are there preferred materials for the walls? | ☐ | ☐ | ☐ |

Comments: _____

_____

| 16. | Are there preferred materials for the floors? | ☐ | ☐ | ☐ |

Comments: _____

_____

| 17. | Are there preferred materials for the ceiling? | ☐ | ☐ | ☐ |

Comments: _____

_____

	YES	NO	N/A

V. Interior Storage

1. Has storage been considered in planning the library? ☐ ☐ ☐
    Comments: _____

    _____

2. Is there a room to store pieces of furniture, equipment, displays, and other miscellaneous items? ☐ ☐ ☐
    Comments: _____

    _____

3. Is there storage space for less frequently used library materials such as old newspapers, periodicals, and donated books awaiting review for possible addition to the collections? ☐ ☐ ☐
    Comments: _____

    _____

4. Is there adequate storage for office and library supplies? ☐ ☐ ☐
    Comments: _____

    _____

5. Is there another building or library property where infrequently used materials can be stored to make room for rapidly growing collections? ☐ ☐ ☐
    Comments: _____

    _____

6. Is there a policy in place to keep the storage area from becoming the library's "attic"? ☐ ☐ ☐
    Comments: _____

    _____

Compliance with ADA Accessibility Guidelines

	YES	NO	N/A

The best source for the latest information about ADA requirements is the U.S. Department of Justice website, ADA Standards for Accessible Design: www.usdoj.gov/crt/ada/adastd94.pdf. This site also provides figures that illustrate many of the following requirements.

A. Transportation, Parking Lots, Parking Signage, and Accessible Routes

1. Is there at least one accessible route within the boundary of the site from a public transportation stop? An accessible route is a continuous, unobstructed path connecting all accessible elements and spaces of a building. Interior accessible routes may include corridors, floors, ramps, elevators, lifts, and clear floor space at fixtures. Exterior accessible routes may include parking access aisles, curb ramps, crosswalks at vehicular ways, walks, ramps, and lifts. ☐ ☐ ☐

   Comments: _____

   _____

2. Are there safe and accessible parking spaces located on the shortest accessible route of travel to an accessible entrance? ☐ ☐ ☐

   Comments: _____

   _____

3. If the building has multiple accessible entrances with adjacent parking, are accessible parking spaces dispersed and located closest to the accessible entrances? ☐ ☐ ☐

   Comments: _____

   _____

		YES	NO	N/A
4.	Do the accessible routes have floors, walks, ramps, stairs, and curb ramps that are stable, firm, and slip resistant?	☐	☐	☐

Comments: _____

_____

5.	Do accessible parking spaces have a designated sign showing the symbol of accessibility?	☐	☐	☐

Comments: _____

_____

6.	Is the minimum clear width of an accessible route at least 36 inches?	☐	☐	☐

Comments: _____

_____

7.	Are the accessible parking spaces at least 8 feet wide and 20 feet long?	☐	☐	☐

Comments: _____

_____

8.	Are the accessible parking lot spaces and aisles level so that wheelchairs will not roll if left unattended while transferring persons to their vehicle?	☐	☐	☐

Comments: _____

_____

9.	Is one in every eight accessible parking spaces, but not less than one overall, served by an access aisle 96 inches in width, with signage that indicates "Van Accessible" under the accessibility symbol?	☐	☐	☐

Comments: _____

_____

10.	Does the facility observe the following requirements for parking spaces?	☐	☐	☐

Number of Spaces	Minimum Accessible Spaces
1 to 25	1
26 to 50	2
51 to 75	3
76 to 100	4
101 to 150	5
151 to 200	6
201 to 300	7
301 to 400	8
401 to 500	9
501 to 1,000	2 percent of total
1,001 and over	20, plus 1 for each 100 over 1,000

Comments: _____

_____

	YES	NO	N/A

11. Are access aisles between van parking spaces 5 feet in width, striped, and part of an accessible route? (Two accessible parking spaces can share a common access aisle.) ☐ ☐ ☐

   Comments: _____

   _____

12. Does the van-accessible parking space clear vertically to at least 9 feet 6 inches high? ☐ ☐ ☐

   Comments: _____

   _____

13. If the library has a passenger-loading zone, does the zone have an access aisle 5 feet wide and 20 feet long, adjacent and parallel to vehicle pull-up space? ☐ ☐ ☐

   Comments: _____

   _____

B. Ground and Floor Surfaces

1. Are slip-resistant floors used throughout the building, and are floor surfaces stable and firm? ☐ ☐ ☐

   Comments: _____

   _____

2. Are changes in vertical level less than ¼ inch? If so, no edge treatment is required. ☐ ☐ ☐

   Comments: _____

   _____

3. Are changes in floor level between ⅓ and ½ inch? If so, the change in the level must be beveled with a slope no greater than 1:2. ☐ ☐ ☐

   Comments: _____

   _____

4. Are changes in level greater than ½ inch? If so, they require a ramp. ☐ ☐ ☐

   Comments: _____

   _____

5. If carpet or carpet tile is used, is it securely attached to the floor, and does it have a firm cushion pad, a level loop, and a maximum pile thickness of less than ½ inch? ☐ ☐ ☐

   Comments: _____

   _____

6. Do gratings located in walking surfaces have spaces no greater than ½ inch in one direction? ☐ ☐ ☐

   Comments: _____

   _____

7. Do gratings have elongated openings? If so, they must be placed so that the long dimension is perpendicular to the dominant direction of travel. ☐ ☐ ☐

   Comments: _____

   _____

	YES	NO	N/A

8. Can an individual with visual disabilities who is using a cane detect objects protruding from the wall or floor?　☐　☐　☐

   Comments: _____

   _____

9. Is there clear and distinct contrast between the floors and walls to assist the visually impaired?　☐　☐　☐

   Comments: _____

   _____

C. Curb Cuts

1. Are there curb cuts or curb ramps at all curbs and walks on accessible routes to accessible entrances?　☐　☐　☐

   Comments: _____

   _____

2. Are there any curbs between the access aisle and the vehicle pull-up space?　☐　☐　☐

   Comments: _____

   _____

3. If so, are there cuts or curb ramps?　☐　☐　☐

   Comments: _____

   _____

4. If there are curb ramps, are they built so they do not extend into vehicle traffic lanes?　☐　☐　☐

   Comments: _____

   _____

5. Is the least possible slope used for every ramp?　☐　☐　☐

   Comments: _____

   _____

6. If a curb ramp is located where pedestrians must walk across the ramp, is it protected by handrails or guardrails?　☐　☐　☐

   Comments: _____

   _____

7. If the curb ramp does not have guardrails, does it have flared sides?　☐　☐　☐

   Comments: _____

   _____

8. Does the curb ramp have a detectable warning extending the full width and depth of the ramp?　☐　☐　☐

   Comments: _____

   _____

	YES	NO	N/A

9. Do curb cuts or curb ramps have a slope of 1:12 or less and flared sides with a slope of 1:10, which is the minimum requirement?   ☐ ☐ ☐

   Comments: _____

10. If the pavement is not level, is the slope no more than 2 percent in all directions?   ☐ ☐ ☐

   Comments: _____

11. Do the curb cuts or curb ramps provide drainage so that water will not be trapped after a storm?   ☐ ☐ ☐

   Comments: _____

12. Are curb cuts or ramps 36 inches wide, excluding the flared sides?   ☐ ☐ ☐

   Comments: _____

13. Are curb ramps at marked crossings wholly contained within the markings, excluding any flared sides?   ☐ ☐ ☐

   Comments: _____

14. If diagonal (or corner-type) curb ramps have returned curbs or other well-defined edges, are they parallel to the direction of pedestrian flow?   ☐ ☐ ☐

   Comments: _____

15. Are any raised islands in crossings cut through level with the street, or do they have curb ramps at both sides and a level area at least 38 inches long between the curb ramps in the part of the island intersected by the crossings?   ☐ ☐ ☐

   Comments: _____

D. Ramps

1. Is the least possible slope used for any ramp? Any part of an accessible route with a slope greater than 1:20 is considered a ramp.   ☐ ☐ ☐

   Comments: _____

2. Is the maximum rise for any ramp less than 30 inches?   ☐ ☐ ☐

   Comments: _____

3. Does the ramp have a minimum clear width of 36 inches?   ☐ ☐ ☐

   Comments: _____

	YES	NO	N/A

4.   Does each ramp have the following?

    a) Level landings at the bottom and top of the ramp and the ramp run   ☐ ☐ ☐

    b) A landing at least as wide as the ramp run leading to it   ☐ ☐ ☐

    c) Landings at least 60 inches in length   ☐ ☐ ☐

    Comments: _____

_____

5.   Does the ramp change direction at landings? If so, the minimum landing size should be 60 inches by 60 inches.   ☐ ☐ ☐

    Comments: _____

_____

6.   Is there a doorway located at a landing? If so, the area in front of the doorway (not automatic or power-assisted) requires a minimum maneuvering clearance of 48 inches.   ☐ ☐ ☐

    Comments: _____

_____

7.   Does the ramp run have a rise greater than 6 inches or a horizontal projection greater than 72 inches? If so, then it requires handrails on both sides.   ☐ ☐ ☐

    Comments: _____

_____

8.   Are the cross slopes of ramp surfaces no greater than 1:50?   ☐ ☐ ☐

    Comments: _____

_____

9.   Are outdoor ramps and their approaches designed so that water will not accumulate on walking surfaces?   ☐ ☐ ☐

    Comments: _____

_____

E.   Stairs

1.   On any given flight of stairs, do all steps have uniform riser heights and uniform tread levels?   ☐ ☐ ☐

    Comments: _____

_____

2.   Are the stair treads no less than 11 inches measured from riser to riser? (Open risers are not permitted.)   ☐ ☐ ☐

    Comments: _____

_____

3.   Is the underside of nosings (the usually rounded edge of a stair) not abrupt?   ☐ ☐ ☐

    Comments: _____

_____

	YES	NO	N/A

4. Is the radius of the curvature at the leading edge of the tread no greater than ½ inch? ☐ ☐ ☐

   Comments: _____

   _____

5. Are the risers sloped at, or do the undersides of the nosings have, an angle not less than 60 degrees from the horizontal? ☐ ☐ ☐

   Comments: _____

   _____

6. Do the stairways have handrails at both sides of the stairs? If so, the handrails should comply with E.5 above. ☐ ☐ ☐

   Comments: _____

   _____

F. Lifts and Elevators

1. If the building has more than one floor, does the wheelchair user have access to an elevator? ☐ ☐ ☐

   Comments: _____

   _____

2. Are accessible elevators on an accessible route? ☐ ☐ ☐

   Comments: _____

   _____

3. Is the elevator operation automatic? ☐ ☐ ☐

   Comments: _____

   _____

4. Do the elevators have an automatic self-leveling feature that will bring the car to floor landings within a tolerance of ½ inch under rated loading to zero loading conditions? This self-leveling feature should be automatic and independent of the operating devices and should correct the over- or under-travel. ☐ ☐ ☐

   Comments: _____

   _____

5. Are call buttons in elevator lobbies and hallways centered at 42 inches above the floor? ☐ ☐ ☐

   Comments: _____

   _____

6. Do the call buttons have a minimum of ¾ inch in the smallest dimension, and is the button designating the up direction placed on top? ☐ ☐ ☐

   Comments: _____

   _____

		YES	NO	N/A

7. Do the call buttons have visual signals to indicate when each call is registered and when each call is answered? ☐ ☐ ☐

Comments: _____

_____

8. Is there a visible and audible signal provided at each hoistway entrance to indicate which car is answering a call? Audible signals should sound once for the up direction and twice for the down direction, or have verbal annunciators that say "up" or "down." ☐ ☐ ☐

Comments: _____

_____

9. Are hall lantern fixtures mounted so that their centerline is at least 72 inches above the lobby floor? ☐ ☐ ☐

Comments: _____

_____

10. Are the signals visible from the vicinity of the hall call button? ☐ ☐ ☐

Comments: _____

_____

11. Do all elevator hoistway entrances have raised and braille floor designations provided on both jambs? The centerline of the characters should be 60 inches above the finished floor, and the characters should be at least 2 inches high. ☐ ☐ ☐

Comments: _____

_____

12. Do elevator doors open and close automatically, and are they provided with a reopening device that will stop automatically if the door becomes obstructed by an object or a person? ☐ ☐ ☐

Comments: _____

_____

13. Are elevator doors open fully in response to a car call for a minimum of three seconds? ☐ ☐ ☐

Comments: _____

_____

14. Does the floor area of elevator cars provide space for a wheelchair user to enter the car, maneuver within reach of the controls, and exit from the car? ☐ ☐ ☐

Comments: _____

_____

15. Is the level of illumination at the car controls, platform, and car threshold and landing sill at least five foot-candles? ☐ ☐ ☐

Comments: _____

_____

	YES	NO	N/A

16. Do elevator car controls consider the following?

    a) Are all control buttons at least ¾ inch in their smallest dimension, and are they raised or flush? ☐ ☐ ☐

    b) Are all control buttons designated by braille and raised standard alphabet characters for letters, arabic characters for numerals, or standard symbols? ☐ ☐ ☐

    c) Are all floor buttons no higher than 54 inches above the finished floor for side approach and 48 inches for front approach? ☐ ☐ ☐

    d) Are emergency controls grouped at the bottom of the panel with their centerlines no less than 35 inches above the finished floor? ☐ ☐ ☐

Comments: _____

_____

17. Is a visual car position indicator provided above the car control panel or over the door to show the position of the elevator in the hoistway? As the car passes or stops at a floor served by the elevators, the corresponding numerals should illuminate, and an audible signal should sound. ☐ ☐ ☐

Comments: _____

_____

18. Is there an emergency two-way communication system between the elevator and a point outside the hoistway? ☐ ☐ ☐

Comments: _____

_____

G. Doors

1. Do doorways have a minimum clear opening of 32 inches with the door open 90 degrees, measured between the face of the door and the opposite stop? ☐ ☐ ☐

Comments: _____

_____

2. Are thresholds raised less than ½ inch from the floor? ☐ ☐ ☐

Comments: _____

_____

3. Does the door allow maneuvering clearance for a person in a wheelchair? Maneuvering room will vary based on type of door. ☐ ☐ ☐

Comments: _____

_____

4. Do handles, pulls, latches, locks, and other operating devices on accessible doors have a shape that is easy to grasp with one hand and does not require tight grasping, tight pinching, or twisting of the wrist to operate? ☐ ☐ ☐

Comments: _____

_____

	YES	NO	N/A

5. Are there easy-to-grip door handles using push-type, lever-operated, or U-type handles?   ☐   ☐   ☐

   Comments: _____

   _____

6. Is hardware required for accessible doors mounted no higher than 48 inches above the finished floor?   ☐   ☐   ☐

   Comments: _____

   _____

7. Do accessible doors allow delay-closing action of at least three seconds to move from an open position of 70 degrees to a point 3 inches from the latch measured to the leading edge of the door?   ☐   ☐   ☐

   Comments: _____

   _____

8. Does the maximum force for pushing or pulling open a door meet the following standards?

   a) *Interior hinged doors:* 5 lbf (A foot-pound [lbf] is a unit measure of torque equal to a pound of force acting perpendicularly to an axis of rotation at a distance of one foot. Also called pound-foot, it is a measure of torque, or the turning power required to open a door.)   ☐   ☐   ☐

   b) *Sliding or folding doors:* 5 lbf   ☐   ☐   ☐

   Comments: _____

   _____

H. Entrances

1. Is a book drop available near the entrance? If so, the handle should be at least 54 inches above the floor for wheelchair approaches from the side. For a forward approach to the book drop, the maximum is 48 inches above the floor to allow reaching from the wheelchair.   ☐   ☐   ☐

   Comments: _____

   _____

2. Are all building entrances accessible to the disabled? Revolving doors or turnstiles should not be the only means of passage at an accessible entrance or along an accessible route.   ☐   ☐   ☐

   Comments: _____

   _____

3. Do all accessible entrance doors display a sign or sticker with the international symbol for accessibility?   ☐   ☐   ☐

   Comments: _____

   _____

	YES	NO	N/A

4. If some entrances are not accessible, are signs displayed directing people to accessible entrances? ☐ ☐ ☐

   Comments: _____

   _____

5. Do library security gates have a clear minimum opening of 32 inches? ☐ ☐ ☐

   Comments: _____

   _____

6. Is there an accessible gate or door provided adjacent to the turnstile or revolving door and is it designed to facilitate the same use pattern? ☐ ☐ ☐

   Comments: _____

   _____

7. Do doorways have a minimum clear opening of 32 inches with the door open 90 degrees? ☐ ☐ ☐

   Comments: _____

   _____

8. Is the minimum space between two hinged or pivoted doors in a series at least 48 inches plus the width of any door swinging into the space? ☐ ☐ ☐

   Comments: _____

   _____

9. Do door thresholds not exceed ¾ inch in height for exterior sliding doors, or ½ inch for other types of doors? ☐ ☐ ☐

   Comments: _____

   _____

10. Do handles, pulls, latches, locks, and other operating devices on accessible doors have a shape that is easy to grasp with one hand and does not require tight grasping, tight pinching, or twisting of the wrist to operate? ☐ ☐ ☐

    • Lever-operated mechanisms, push-type mechanisms, and U-shaped handles are acceptable designs.

    • Hardware required for accessible door opening should be mounted no higher than 48 inches.

    Comments: _____

    _____

11. If a door has a closer, is it adjusted so that from an open position of 70 degrees, the door will take at least three seconds to move to a point 3 inches from the latch, measured to the leading edge of the door? ☐ ☐ ☐

    Comments: _____

    _____

12. Is the maximum force for pushing or pulling open a door as follows?

    a) *Fire doors:* the minimum opening force allowable by the appropriate administrative authority ☐ ☐ ☐

    b) *Interior hinged doors and sliding or folding doors:* a maximum force of 5 lbf ☐ ☐ ☐

    Comments: _____

    _____

	YES	NO	N/A

I. Accessible Routes within the Building

1. Is there at least one accessible route connecting accessible buildings, facilities, elements, and spaces? An accessible route is a continuous, unobstructed path connecting all accessible elements and spaces of a building. Interior accessible routes may include corridors, floors, ramps, elevators, lifts, and clear floor space at fixtures. ☐ ☐ ☐

   Comments: _____

   _____

2. Is the minimum clear width of an accessible route 36 inches except at doorways? If a person in a wheelchair must make a turn around an obstruction, does the minimum clear width allow this to take place? Usually this is 60 inches by 60 inches. ☐ ☐ ☐

   Comments: _____

   _____

3. If the accessible route is less than 5 feet in width, are there passing spaces of 5 feet at intervals of not more than 200 feet? ☐ ☐ ☐

   Comments: _____

   _____

4. Is there headroom clearance of at least 80 inches above the floor along accessible routes? ☐ ☐ ☐

   Comments: _____

   _____

5. Are there protruding objects (e.g., telephones, drinking fountains, and/or furniture) along these travel routes? ☐ ☐ ☐

   Comments: _____

   _____

6. If there are any protruding objects with their leading edges at or below 27 inches above the floor, do they leave a clear minimum path of 36 inches? ☐ ☐ ☐

   Comments: _____

   _____

7. Are ground and floor surfaces stable, firm, and slip-resistant? ☐ ☐ ☐

   Comments: _____

   _____

8. Does any accessible route serving any accessible space or element serve as a means of egress for emergencies or connect to an accessible area of rescue assistance? ☐ ☐ ☐

   Comments: _____

   _____

YES   NO   N/A

J. Drinking Fountains

1. Are the spouts on all drinking fountains no higher than 36 inches measured from the floor to the spout outlet?

    □   □   □

    Comments: _____

2. Are the spouts of drinking fountains and water coolers at the front of the unit, and do they direct the flow in a trajectory that is parallel or nearly parallel to the front of the unit?

    □   □   □

    Comments: _____

3. Does the water flow at least 4 inches high above the spout so a cup or glass can be placed under the water flow?

    □   □   □

    Comments: _____

4. If the drinking fountain is a round or an oval bowl, is the spout positioned so the edge of the water is within 3 inches of the front of the fountain?

    □   □   □

    Comments: _____

5. Are controls front mounted or, if side mounted, near the front edge?

    □   □   □

    Comments: _____

6. Are controls and operating mechanisms operable with one hand without tight grasping, tight pinching, or twisting of the wrist?

    □   □   □

    Comments: _____

7. If the accessible water fountain is wall or post mounted and has knee space, is the space at least 27 inches high, 30 inches wide, and 17 to 19 inches deep?

    □   □   □

    Comments: _____

8. Does the above water fountain have a minimum clear floor space of 30 inches by 48 inches to allow a person in a wheelchair to approach the unit facing forward?

    □   □   □

    Comments: _____

9. Do freestanding or built-in drinking fountains have a clear floor space of at least 30 inches by 48 inches that allows a person in a wheelchair to make parallel approaches to the unit?

    □   □   □

    Comments: _____

	YES	NO	N/A

K. Water Closets

1. Do water closets (WCs) not located in stalls and centered on the wall with direct access have a 48-inch minimum entrance, a 66-inch clear floor space in front of the water closet, and a 36-inch minimum space on the wall behind the water closet?   ☐   ☐   ☐

    Comments: _____

    _____

2. Do WCs not located in stalls and located on one side of the rear wall with direct access have a 60-inch minimum entrance, a 56-inch clear floor space in front of the WC, and a 60-inch minimum space on the wall behind the WC?   ☐   ☐   ☐

    Comments: _____

    _____

3. For WCs not located in stalls, are there grab bars 33 to 36 inches on center above the floor and a minimum of 42 inches in length?   ☐   ☐   ☐

    Comments: _____

    _____

4. Is the height of the WC between 17 and 19 inches measured at the top of the toilet seat? Seats should not be spring-loaded to return to a lifted position.   ☐   ☐   ☐

    Comments: _____

    _____

5. Are flush controls operated by hand or automatically? _____

    _____

    Comments: _____

    _____

6. Are controls for flush valves mounted on the wide side of toilet areas no more than 44 inches above the floor?   ☐   ☐   ☐

    Comments: _____

    _____

7. Are toilet paper dispensers installed within reach and located 19 inches above the floor?   ☐   ☐   ☐

    Comments: _____

    _____

8. Are other fixtures in the restroom (soap dispensers, towels, auto-dryers, sanitary-napkin dispensers, wastepaper receptacles, etc.) located so the controls or dispensers are at a maximum of 48 inches from the floor?   ☐   ☐   ☐

    Comments: _____

    _____

9. Are coat and purse hooks at a height of approximately 48 inches to make them convenient to wheelchair users?   ☐   ☐   ☐

    Comments: _____

    _____

YES   NO   N/A

L. Toilet Rooms

1. Are there signs indicating the nearest accessible toilet room available for persons with disabilities?   ☐   ☐   ☐

    Comments: _____

    _____

2. Is there at least one toilet room accessible for persons with disabilities?   ☐   ☐   ☐

    Comments: _____

    _____

3. Is the toilet room marked with braille signage?   ☐   ☐   ☐

    Comments: _____

    _____

4. Is the door into the toilet room easily opened by the disabled? See section G (doors) in this chapter for requirements.   ☐   ☐   ☐

    Comments: _____

    _____

M. Toilet Stalls

1. Is at least one stall accessible to a wheelchair, and does it display the international symbol of accessibility?   ☐   ☐   ☐

    Comments: _____

    _____

2. Is the accessible toilet stall on an accessible route?   ☐   ☐   ☐

    Comments: _____

    _____

3. Are there 60 inches of clear floor space in the restroom for a wheelchair to make a 180-degree turn?   ☐   ☐   ☐

    Comments: _____

    _____

4. Does the immediate area allow 48 inches of clear space to approach the stall door?   ☐   ☐   ☐

    Comments: _____

    _____

5. Is there a minimum clearance of 36 inches between all fixtures to an accessible stall?   ☐   ☐   ☐

    Comments: _____

    _____

6. Do WCs in accessible stalls meet the requirements listed above for water closets?   ☐   ☐   ☐

    Comments: _____

		YES	NO	N/A
7.	Are stall doors at least 36 inches wide?	☐	☐	☐
	Comments: _____			
	_____			
8.	Does the door of the stall open out?	☐	☐	☐
	Comments: _____			
	_____			
9.	Do standard toilet stalls have a minimum depth of 56 inches for a wall-mounted WC and 59 inches for a floor-mounted WC?	☐	☐	☐
	Comments: _____			
	_____			
10.	Is there a toe clearance of at least 9 inches above the floor for standard stalls? If the depth of the stall is greater than 60 inches, toe clearance is not required.	☐	☐	☐
	Comments: _____			
	_____			
11.	Is the toilet-paper holder located within easy reach from the toilet and at least 19 inches from the floor, with continuous paper flow?	☐	☐	☐
	Comments: _____			
	_____			
12.	Are coat and purse hooks at a height of approximately 48 inches to make them convenient to wheelchair users?	☐	☐	☐
	Comments: _____			
	_____			
13.	Are there grab bars located in the stall, and do they meet the requirements listed for grab bars below (see section P of this chapter)?	☐	☐	☐
	Comments: _____			
	_____			

N. Urinals

		YES	NO	N/A
1.	Is the rim of the accessible urinal no more than 17 inches above the floor?	☐	☐	☐
	Comments: _____			
	_____			
2.	Is there a clear space of at least 30 by 48 inches in front of the urinals?	☐	☐	☐
	Comments: _____			
	_____			
3.	Are flush controls either hand operated or automatic, and mounted no more than 44 inches off the floor?	☐	☐	☐
	Comments: _____			
	_____			

	YES	NO	N/A

4. Are the controls and operating mechanisms capable of being operated with one hand and without requiring tight grasping, tight pinching, or twisting of the wrist? ☐ ☐ ☐

Comments: _____

_____

5. Is the force required to activate the controls no greater than 5 lbf? ☐ ☐ ☐

Comments: _____

_____

O. Lavatories

1. Is there a clear floor space 30 by 48 inches in front of a lavatory to allow a forward approach? ☐ ☐ ☐

Comments: _____

_____

2. Does the clear floor space adjoin or overlap an accessible route and extend a maximum of 19 inches underneath the lavatory? ☐ ☐ ☐

Comments: _____

_____

3. Are lavatories mounted with the rim or counter surface no more than 34 inches above the finished floor? ☐ ☐ ☐

Comments: _____

_____

4. Is there a clearance space under the lavatory 29 inches above the finished floor to the bottom of the lavatory apron? ☐ ☐ ☐

Comments: _____

_____

5. Is the knee clearance under the lavatory a minimum of 8 inches and the toe clearance 6 inches? The total distance from the front lip of the lavatory to the wall should be a minimum of 17 inches. ☐ ☐ ☐

Comments: _____

_____

6. Is the depth of the sink a maximum of 6½ inches? ☐ ☐ ☐

Comments: _____

_____

7. Are hot water and drain pipes either insulated or enclosed to protect against contact? ☐ ☐ ☐

Comments: _____

_____

	YES	NO	N/A
8. Are faucets operable with one hand? Lever-operated, push-type, and electronically controlled mechanisms are examples of acceptable design.	☐	☐	☐
Comments: _____			
9. If self-closing valves are used in faucets, do they remain open for at least ten seconds?	☐	☐	☐
Comments: _____			
10. Can faucets be operated with no more than 5 lbf?	☐	☐	☐
Comments: _____			
11. Are mirrors mounted with the bottom edge of the reflective surface no more than 40 inches above the floor?	☐	☐	☐
Comments: _____			

P. Handrails and Grab Bars

	YES	NO	N/A
1. Are all handrails and grab bars accessible?	☐	☐	☐
Comments: _____			
2. Are handrails installed along both sides of ramp segments? The inside handrail on switchback or dogleg ramps should always be continuous.	☐	☐	☐
Comments: _____			
3. If handrails are not continuous, do they extend at least 12 inches beyond the top and bottom of the ramp segment parallel with the floor or ground surface?	☐	☐	☐
Comments: _____			
4. Are the handrail gripping surfaces mounted between 35 and 38 inches above ramp surfaces?	☐	☐	☐
Comments: _____			
5. Is the clear space between the handrail and the wall 1 to 1½ inches?	☐	☐	☐
Comments: _____			
6. Are handrails and grab bars between 1¼ and 1½ inches in diameter?	☐	☐	☐
Comments: _____			

	YES	NO	N/A

7. Are gripping surfaces continuous?   ☐ ☐ ☐

    Comments: _____

    _____

8. Are the ends of handrails either rounded or returned smoothly to floor, wall, or post? ☐   ☐   ☐

    Comments: _____

    _____

9. Are handrails and grab bars secure in their fittings? They should not rotate within
    their fittings.   ☐ ☐ ☐

    Comments: _____

    _____

10. Are grab bars placed appropriately and where required, adjacent to WCs, toilet
    stalls, and urinals?   ☐ ☐ ☐

    Comments: _____

    _____

11. Is there a grab bar on the wall closest to the WC, 40 inches in length, 33 to
    36 inches from the floor, and 12 inches from the back wall?   ☐ ☐ ☐

    Comments: _____

    _____

12. Are there at least 1½ inches of space between the grab bar and the wall?   ☐ ☐ ☐

    Comments: _____

    _____

13. Are grab bars capable of resisting a force of 250 lbf?   ☐ ☐ ☐

    Comments: _____

    _____

14. Are grab bars free of sharp, abrasive, or protruding elements?   ☐ ☐ ☐

    Comments: _____

    _____

Q. Controls and Operating Mechanisms

1. Are all controls and operating mechanisms accessible?   ☐ ☐ ☐

    Comments: _____

    _____

2. Is there clear floor space at least 30 by 48 inches provided in front of the controls,
    dispensers, receptacles, and other operable equipment mechanisms to allow
    a forward approach by a person in a wheelchair, and is the clear space on an
    accessible route?   ☐ ☐ ☐

    Comments: _____

    _____

	YES	NO	N/A

3. Is the highest operable part of the controls, dispensers, receptacles, and other operable equipment placed within a maximum of 48 inches?   ☐ ☐ ☐

Comments: _____

_____

4. Are electrical and communications system receptacles on walls mounted no less than 15 inches above the floor?   ☐ ☐ ☐

Comments: _____

_____

5. Are controls and operating mechanisms operable with one hand without requiring tight grasping, tight pinching, or twisting of the wrist?   ☐ ☐ ☐

Comments: _____

_____

6. Is the force required to activate controls no greater than 5 lbf?   ☐ ☐ ☐

Comments: _____

_____

R. Alarms

1. Are all alarm systems accessible?   ☐ ☐ ☐

Comments: _____

_____

2. At a minimum, are visual signal appliances provided in restrooms and other general-use areas (meeting rooms, hallways, lobbies, and any other area for common use)?   ☐ ☐ ☐

Comments: _____

_____

3. If provided, do audible emergency alarms produce a sound that exceeds the prevailing ambient sound in the room or space by at least 15 dBA, or exceeds any maximum sound level with a duration of 60 seconds by 5 dBA? The decibel (dB) is used to measure sound level; the A scale is the most frequently used sound level filter. Measurements made on this scale are expressed as dBA.   ☐ ☐ ☐

Comments: _____

_____

4. Is the sound level of the emergency alarm below 120 dBA?   ☐ ☐ ☐

Comments: _____

_____

5. Is the visual alarm system integrated into the building or facility alarm system?   ☐ ☐ ☐

Comments: _____

_____

	YES	NO	N/A

6. Do the visual alarm signals have the following minimum photometric and location features?

a) A xenon strobe-type lamp or equivalent ☐ ☐ ☐

b) A color that is clear or nominal white (i.e., unfiltered or clear filtered white light) ☐ ☐ ☐

c) A maximum pulse duration of $\frac{2}{10}$ of one second (0.2 sec) with a maximum duty cycle of 40 percent. The pulse duration is defined as the time interval between initial and final points of 10 percent of maximum signal. ☐ ☐ ☐

d) A flash rate of a minimum of 1 Hz and a maximum of 3 Hz ☐ ☐ ☐

e) Placement 80 inches above the highest floor level within the space of 6 inches below the ceiling, whichever is lower ☐ ☐ ☐

f) Location such that no place in any room or space is more than 50 feet from the signal ☐ ☐ ☐

Comments: _____

_____

S. Signage

1. Do all signs designating permanent rooms and spaces in the building comply with the ADA Accessibility Guidelines for Buildings and Facilities (ADAAG)? ☐ ☐ ☐

Comments: _____

_____

2. Is large, clearly printed signage provided to identify all areas and functions in the library for the hearing and visually impaired? ☐ ☐ ☐

Comments: _____

_____

3. Does directional and informational signage about functional spaces in the building comply with ADAAG? ☐ ☐ ☐

Comments: _____

_____

4. Do all accessible elements (i.e., entrance doors, restrooms, water fountains, and parking spaces) display the international symbol of accessibility? ☐ ☐ ☐

Comments: _____

_____

5. Are the signs placed perpendicular to the route of travel? ☐ ☐ ☐

Comments: _____

_____

6. Can permanent signs be approached without encountering a protruding object or standing within the swing of a door? ☐ ☐ ☐

Comments: _____

_____

	YES	NO	N/A

7. Do letters and numbers on signs have a width-to-height ratio between 3:5 and 1:1 and a stroke-width-to-height ratio between 1:5 and 1:10? ☐ ☐ ☐

Comments: _____

8. Are characters and numbers on signs sized according to the viewing distance from which they are to be read? The minimum heights are measured using an uppercase X. Lowercase characters are permitted. ☐ ☐ ☐

Comments: _____

9. Are letters and numbers raised ⅓₂ inch in uppercase sans serif and accompanied with Grade 2 braille? Raised characters should be at least ⅝ inch high, but no higher than 2 inches. ☐ ☐ ☐

Comments: _____

10. Are pictograms accompanied by the equivalent verbal description placed directly below the pictogram? ☐ ☐ ☐

Comments: _____

11. Is the border dimension of the pictogram 6 inches minimum in height? ☐ ☐ ☐

Comments: _____

12. Are the characters and backgrounds of permanent signs constructed with a matte, nonglare, eggshell-colored, or some other nonglare finish? ☐ ☐ ☐

Comments: _____

13. Do characters and symbols contrast with their background—either light characters on a dark background or dark characters on a light background? ☐ ☐ ☐

Comments: _____

14. Are permanent signs for rooms and spaces installed on the wall adjacent to the latch side of the door and mounted at 60 inches above the finished floor to the centerline of the sign? ☐ ☐ ☐

Comments: _____

15. Is the mounting location for the signage above such that a person may approach within 3 inches of the signage without encountering protruding objects or standing within the swing of a door? ☐ ☐ ☐

Comments: _____

	YES	NO	N/A

16. Are the following international symbols of accessibility displayed (the website ADA Standards for Accessible Design has illustrations of the signs)?

   a) Volume-control telephones have a volume control identified by a sign depicting a telephone handset with radiating sound waves. ☐ ☐ ☐

   b) Text telephones are identified by directional signage indicating the location of the nearest text telephone placed adjacent to all banks of telephones that do not contain a text telephone. The sign must display the international TDD symbol. ☐ ☐ ☐

   c) The availability of assistive listening systems is identified by a sign that includes the international symbol of access for hearing loss. ☐ ☐ ☐

Comments: _____

_____

T. Telephones

1. Are public telephones identified by the international symbol of accessibility? ☐ ☐ ☐

   Comments: _____

_____

2. Are public telephones accessible by providing a clear floor or ground space at least 30 by 48 inches that allows either a forward or parallel approach by a person using a wheelchair? ☐ ☐ ☐

   Comments: _____

_____

3. Do bases, enclosures, and fixed seats allow unimpeded approaches to telephones by people who use wheelchairs? ☐ ☐ ☐

   Comments: _____

_____

4. Is the highest operable part of the telephone placed at an accessible height (48 inches) for wheelchair users? ☐ ☐ ☐

   Comments: _____

_____

5. Do hearing-aid-compatible and volume-control telephones

   a) Have volume controls capable of a minimum of 12 dBA above normal? ☐ ☐ ☐

   b) Have push-button controls? ☐ ☐ ☐

   Comments: _____

_____

6. Is the cord length from the telephone to the handset a minimum of 29 inches? ☐ ☐ ☐

   Comments: _____

_____

	YES	NO	N/A

7. If telephone books are provided, are they located within the 48-inch accessible height? ☐ ☐ ☐

Comments: _____

_____

8. If text telephones are used with a pay telephone, are they permanently affixed within or adjacent to the telephone enclosure? ☐ ☐ ☐

Comments: _____

_____

9. Are pay telephones designed to accommodate a portable text telephone equipped with a shelf and an electrical outlet within or adjacent to the telephone enclosure? ☐ ☐ ☐

Comments: _____

_____

10. Is the telephone handset capable of being placed flush on the surface of the shelf? ☐ ☐ ☐

Comments: _____

_____

11. If pay telephones are not provided with the above accessible features, is an equivalent facilitation system provided at a service desk when the library is open? ☐ ☐ ☐

Comments: _____

_____

U. Fixed or Built-in Seating and Tables

1. Do at least 5 percent, or a minimum of one of each element, of fixed seats, tables, or study carrels have access for people with disabilities? ☐ ☐ ☐

Comments: _____

_____

2. Is there clear space of at least 30 by 48 inches for people in wheelchairs in front of fixed tables and study carrels? This allows either a forward or parallel approach by a person using a wheelchair. ☐ ☐ ☐

Comments: _____

_____

3. Is there a knee clearance of 27 inches high, 30 inches wide, and 19 inches deep for people in wheelchairs in front of fixed tables and study carrels? ☐ ☐ ☐

Comments: _____

_____

4. Are the tops of tables and study carrel counters between 28 and 34 inches above the finished floor or ground? ☐ ☐ ☐

Comments: _____

_____

	YES	NO	N/A

5. Do circulation, reference, and other service desks meet code requirements designated for built-in tables and counters?

   a) Is the height of the countertop between 28 and 34 inches above the finished floor? For the circulation desk, the 34-inch dimension is preferred. ☐ ☐ ☐

   b) Is knee clearance at least 27 inches high? For the staff side of the desk, there should be a 19-inch-deep knee clearance space. ☐ ☐ ☐

   c) Is the minimum clear area for a person in a wheelchair approaching the desk 36 inches wide? ☐ ☐ ☐

   Comments: _____

_____

6. Does at least one lane at each checkout area meet the requirements for an accessible route? ☐ ☐ ☐

   Comments: _____

_____

7. Is the minimum clear aisle space at card catalogs, OPAC desks, and magazine displays 36 inches, with a maximum reach height of 48 inches? ☐ ☐ ☐

   Comments: _____

_____

8. Are aisles for book stacks (storage of library materials) a minimum of 36 inches wide (42 inches preferred)? ☐ ☐ ☐

   Comments: _____

_____

9. Are aisles for bookshelves (storage of commonly used publications such as current periodicals and frequently used reference materials) 44 inches minimum? ☐ ☐ ☐

   Comments: _____

_____

10. Is assistance available to retrieve books off shelves? If so, there is no height limit. ☐ ☐ ☐

   Comments: _____

_____

11. If assistance is not available, is topmost-shelf height limited to 54 inches? ☐ ☐ ☐

   Comments: _____

_____

V. Assembly Areas

1. Are wheelchair locations an integral part of any library fixed-seating plan in meeting and assembly rooms so as to provide people with physical disabilities a line of sight comparable to those members of the general public using the facility? ☐ ☐ ☐

   Comments: _____

_____

	YES	NO	N/A

2. Is the meeting room or assembly area served by an accessible route? ☐ ☐ ☐
    Comments: _____

    _____

3. Does the facility observe the following capacity for wheelchair locations? ☐ ☐ ☐

Room Capacity	Minimum Accessible Spaces
4 to 25	1
26 to 50	2
51 to 300	4
301 to 500	6
Over 500	6, plus 1 additional space for each seating capacity increase of 100.

    When the seating capacity exceeds 300, wheelchair spaces should be provided in more than one location.

    Comments: _____

    _____

4. Does each wheelchair location provide minimum clear ground or floor space 36 inches wide by 48 inches for forward or rear access and 66 inches minimum for side access? ☐ ☐ ☐
    Comments: _____

    _____

5. Is the floor surface in the meeting room or assembly room stable, firm, and slip-resistant? ☐ ☐ ☐
    Comments: _____

    _____

6. Does the meeting room provide an assistive listening system to augment standard public address and audio systems? ☐ ☐ ☐
    Comments: _____

    _____

7. If the meeting room has fixed seating, is the assistive listening system located within a 50-foot viewing distance of the stage or front area? ☐ ☐ ☐
    Comments: _____

    _____

8. Does the signage include the international symbol of accessibility for the hearing impaired to notify patrons of the availability of a listening system? ☐ ☐ ☐
    Comments: _____

    _____

W. Building Assistance Facilities

1. Is there a designated rescue assistance area in the facility? ☐ ☐ ☐
    Comments: _____

    _____

		YES	NO	N/A
2.	Are there designated emergency routes in the facility?	☐	☐	☐
	Comments: _____			
	_____			
3.	Are these routes easily identified?	☐	☐	☐
	Comments: _____			
	_____			
4.	Are there signs to guide users in case of emergency?	☐	☐	☐
	Comments: _____			
	_____			
5.	Are the signs illuminated?	☐	☐	☐
	Comments: _____			
	_____			
6.	Do these signs point the way to the rescue assistance area?	☐	☐	☐
	Comments: _____			
	_____			
7.	Is the rescue assistance area enclosed, smoke-proof, and vented to the outside?	☐	☐	☐
	Comments: _____			
	_____			
8.	Is the rescue assistance area separated from the building interior by at least one fire-resistant door?	☐	☐	☐
	Comments: _____			
	_____			
9.	Does the rescue assistance area provide at least two accessible 30-by-48-inch wheelchair spaces that do not encroach on the width of any required exit route?	☐	☐	☐
	Comments: _____			
	_____			
10.	Is there a two-way communication system between the primary entrance and the rescue assistance area?	☐	☐	☐
	Comments: _____			
	_____			

Telecommunications, Electrical, and Miscellaneous Equipment

	YES	NO	N/A

Some of the material in this chapter is based on the ANSI/TIA/EIA-568-B and ANSI/TIA/EIA-569-B Standards.

A. General Considerations

1. Are electrical power outlets and data outlets planned for all areas where electronic workstations will be located? ☐ ☐ ☐

   Comments: _____

   _____

2. Is a wireless system planned with wireless access points? Wireless access points (AP or WAP) are specially configured nodes on wireless local area networks (WLAN). Access points act as central transmitters and receivers of WLAN radio signals. ☐ ☐ ☐

   Comments: _____

   _____

3. Are workstations located and grouped to enhance noise control and privacy? ☐ ☐ ☐

   Comments: _____

   _____

4. Has equipment been selected with quiet operation in mind? ☐ ☐ ☐

   Comments: _____

   _____

	YES	NO	N/A

B. Telecommunications Entrances and Closets

1. Is the building entrance facility (the point at which outside cabling interfaces with the interior building backbone cabling) a locked, dedicated, and enclosed room with a plywood termination field provided on two walls? (The plywood should be ¾ inch, with dimensions 8 feet high by 39 inches wide.)   ☐ ☐ ☐

   Comments: _____

2. Is there an equipment room (essentially a large telecommunications closet) that houses the main distribution frame, PBXs, secondary voltage protection, etc.? The equipment room is often appended to the entrance facilities or a computer room to allow shared air-conditioning, security, fire control, lighting, and limited access.   ☐ ☐ ☐

   Comments: _____

3. Does the room have at least 150 square feet of floor space? The rule of thumb is to provide 0.75 square feet of equipment room floor space for every 100 square feet of user workstation area.   ☐ ☐ ☐

   Comments: _____

4. Is the room located away from sources of electromagnetic interference (transformers, motors, induction heaters, theft detection systems, etc.) until interference is less than 3 V/m (volt per meter-unit of electrical strength) across the frequency spectrum?   ☐ ☐ ☐

   Comments: _____

5. Is the room in an area that is not subject to floods?   ☐ ☐ ☐

   Comments: _____

6. Are all surfaces treated to reduce dust, and walls and ceilings painted white or pastel to improve visibility?   ☐ ☐ ☐

   Comments: _____

7. Are there single or double (36-by-80-inch) lockable doors in order to limit access to the room?   ☐ ☐ ☐

   Comments: _____

8. Has piping, ductwork, mechanical equipment, power cabling, and unrelated storage been kept out of the equipment room?   ☐ ☐ ☐

   Comments: _____

	YES	NO	N/A

9. Is the room maintained 24 hours per day, 365 days per year, at a temperature of 64 to 75 degrees Fahrenheit, 30 to 55 percent humidity, with positive pressure? ☐ ☐ ☐

Comments: _____

_____

10. Is there a minimum of two dedicated 15 A/100 VAC (amps per volts of alternating current) duplex outlets on separate circuits? ☐ ☐ ☐

Comments: _____

_____

11. Are there convenience duplex outlets placed at 6-foot intervals around the perimeter of the room? ☐ ☐ ☐

Comments: _____

_____

12. Has an emergency power system been considered? ☐ ☐ ☐

Comments: _____

_____

13. If the equipment room is more than 300 feet from a service point, have additional telecommunications closets been included? (The recommended size is 10 by 11 feet for each 10,000-square-foot area served.) ☐ ☐ ☐

Comments: _____

_____

14. Is there a 24-hour security system installed? ☐ ☐ ☐

Comments: _____

_____

15. Is there a separate fire suppression system? ☐ ☐ ☐

Comments: _____

_____

C. Horizontal Pathways

Horizontal pathways extend between the telecommunications closet and the work area. A variety of generic pathway options are available. Have the following horizontal pathways been considered? (Options depend on the design of the building.)

1. Plenum ceiling. (Cable bundles run from the telecom closet along J-hooks suspended above a plenum ceiling, fan out when a work zone is reached, drop through interior walls or support columns or raceways, and terminate at an information outlet, or I/O.) ☐ ☐ ☐

Comments: _____

_____

	YES	NO	N/A

2. Under-floor duct. (Single- or dual-level rectangular ducts are embedded in greater than 2.5-inch-thick concrete flooring.)   ☐ ☐ ☐

   Comments: _____

   _____

3. Flush duct. (A single-level rectangular duct is embedded flush in greater than 1-inch-thick concrete flooring.)   ☐ ☐ ☐

   Comments: _____

   _____

4. Multichannel raceway. (Cellular raceway ducts capable of routing telecom and power cabling separately are embedded in greater than 3-inch-thick reinforced concrete.)   ☐ ☐ ☐

   Comments: _____

   _____

5. Cellular floor. (Preformed hollows, or steel-lined cells, are provided in concrete, with header ducts from the telecom closet arranged at right angles to the cells.)   ☐ ☐ ☐

   Comments: _____

   _____

6. Trench duct. (A wide, solid tray, sometimes divided into compartments and fitted with a flat top with gaskets along its entire length, is embedded flush with the concrete finish.)   ☐ ☐ ☐

   Comments: _____

   _____

7. Access floor. (Modular floor panels, supported by pedestals, are used in computer rooms and equipment rooms.)   ☐ ☐ ☐

   Comments: _____

   _____

8. Conduit. (This option is used only when outlet locations are permanent, device density is low, and flexibility for future changes is not required.)   ☐ ☐ ☐

   Comments: _____

   _____

9. Perimeter pathways. (This option includes surface, recessed, molding, and multichannel raceways.)   ☐ ☐ ☐

   Comments: _____

   _____

YES   NO   N/A

D. Cabling and Outlets

1. Is a star topology structured cabling system used. In a star topology, each work-area telecommunications outlet is connected to a cross-connect in a telecommunications closet. All cables from a floor or an area in the building therefore run back to one central point for administration. Each telecommunications closet must be star wired back to the equipment room for the building.   ☐   ☐   ☐

    Comments: _____

    _____

2. Is the structured cabling system compatible with the type of media to be used?   ☐   ☐   ☐

    Comments: _____

    _____

3. Based on the media to be transmitted, what cable alternatives have been selected?

    a) *Category 5 cable.* The minimum requirement should be unshielded twisted pair (UTP) N4-pair, 24-gauge, 100 ohm copper cable. (Unshielded twisted pair cables closely resemble telephone cables but are enhanced for data communications to allow higher-frequency transmissions. Category 5 cables and connection hardware are the minimum usually required. They are rated up to 100 MHz and are designed to handle any current copper-based application for voice, video, or data.)   ☐   ☐   ☐

    b) *Category 6 cable.* Category 6 is now the suggested standard. It is similar to Category 5E, except that it is made to a higher standard and provides performance of up to 250 MHz, more than double Category 5 and 5E.   ☐   ☐   ☐

    c) *Single-mode and multi-mode optical fiber cables.* The highest-performing structured cabling systems use fiber optics and will be the choice of most libraries in the long run as fiber costs decline.   ☐   ☐   ☐

    Comments: _____

    _____

4. Does each workstation have a minimum of two information outlet ports?   ☐   ☐   ☐

    Comments: _____

    _____

5. Is every seat in the library considered a workstation and equipped with telecommunications outlets? (A minimum requirement is one outlet port for voice and one for data.)   ☐   ☐   ☐

    Comments: _____

    _____

YES   NO   N/A

E. Wireless Technology

1. Will the library provide customers with a wireless network for access to the Internet
    and library databases? A wireless network uses radio waves to provide communication
    and may be used by library customers to access the Internet and library materials
    through library wireless workstations, and/or through their own personal computers
    if they are equipped to receive wireless signals.   ☐   ☐   ☐

    - Wireless access uses the Wi-Fi standard (also known as IEEE 802.11b, g, or n). Most users can simply bring
      their wireless-enabled laptop computer or other wireless device to the library and turn it on. The computer
      will automatically recognize the wireless network.

    - Wireless access points (WAP or AP) located throughout the library communicate with customers' wireless
      devices almost anywhere in the building. When a customer's wireless network card senses a signal, a message
      appears on his or her screen indicating a wireless network is available. Before connection is allowed, customers
      should be asked if they abide by the library's Internet Public Use Policy and Guidelines. Usually if they click that
      they agree, they may use the service immediately.

    - Library wireless electronic workstations are usually connected at all times.

    - Wireless connectivity is usually slower than wired connections and there may be instances when the need for
      higher bandwidth makes using a wired connection preferable. However, for many applications, such as web
      browsing and e-mail, wireless connectivity should be sufficient.

    - Some researchers have found that current wireless protocols can be compromised using certain available hacking
      tools. An intruder can "listen in" on wireless traffic, and library users should be made aware of this potential issue.

    Comments: _____

2. Has care been taken in locating wireless access points or nodes in the library?
    Wireless telecommunications networks require significant effort in placing nodes
    or access points within the library to ensure proper wireless coverage for users in
    the library. Placement is both an art and a science. The access points will tie back
    to switches via Ethernet. Each access point requires a minimum of 10 Mbps (Mbps
    stands for millions of bits per second or megabits per second and is a measure of
    bandwidth, the total information flow over a given time on a telecommunications
    medium). An 802.11g WLAN offers theoretical bandwidth up to 54 Mbps. (In
    contrast, typical wired Ethernets run at 100 Mbps.)   ☐   ☐   ☐

    Comments: _____

3. In placing WAP for users, consider the following issues:

    a) Have access points been designed to give the best signal to the most users
       or coverage area?   ☐   ☐   ☐

    b) If not, has a minimum number of access points been determined that will
       ensure that every user or area gets a minimum signal or better? Signals
       are shared, so the more users per WAP, the smaller each user's share of the
       bandwidth will be.   ☐   ☐   ☐

    c) Has distance been minimized based on the design objective above? Distance
       is key, because data rates go down as distance increases.   ☐   ☐   ☐

	YES	NO	N/A
d) Does each potential AP have access to power and Ethernet cables?	☐	☐	☐
e) Have the maximum cable length limitations (100 meters) for the cable running from the Ethernet switch to the access point been taken into account? If a 100-meter cable won't reach your preferred access point location, think about moving the access point or possibly using a WLAN bridge or optical fiber to make the connection.	☐	☐	☐
f) Is the physical access point or node as far out of reach as possible—preferably on or above the ceiling (depending on construction)? Some users want a physical indication of nodes so that they may locate near one.	☐	☐	☐

Comments: _____

_____

4. Has a radio frequency (RF) site survey been done before installing the access points? The site survey will spot potential sources of RF interference and provide a basis for determining the most effective installation locations for access points. ☐ ☐ ☐

   - The ultimate goal of an RF site survey is to supply enough information to determine the number and placement of access points that provides adequate coverage throughout the building.

   - An RF site survey also detects the presence of interference coming from other sources that could degrade the performance of the wireless LAN.

Comments: _____

_____

5. Have the following steps been taken in conducting the RF site survey?

	YES	NO	N/A
a) Have potential locations for AP been plotted from a building floor plan and tentatively laid out on the plan?	☐	☐	☐
b) Has a visual inspection been done by walking through the facility before performing any tests to verify the accuracy of the facility diagram? This is a good time to note any potential barriers that may impact RF signals.	☐	☐	☐
c) Have user areas been identified and plotted on the facility diagram?	☐	☐	☐
d) Have preliminary access point locations been determined? By considering the location of wireless users and range estimations of the wireless LAN products you're using, approximate the locations of access points that will provide adequate coverage throughout the user areas and plan on some overlap.	☐	☐	☐
e) Have mounting locations been considered that will provide the best signal for the AP? These might be vertical posts or supports above ceiling tiles. Be sure to recognize suitable locations for installing the access points, antennas, data cables, and power lines.	☐	☐	☐
f) Have the sites been tested for data rate, signal strength, and signal quality using commercially available software? Install an access point at each preliminary location, and monitor the site survey software readings by walking varying distances away from the access point.	☐	☐	☐
g) If the site meets the data rate, signal strength, and signal quality requirements, has the AP been installed?	☐	☐	☐

YES   NO   N/A

h) Have the final locations been documented on the building plan? This is vital for future remodeling.   ☐   ☐   ☐

Comments: _____

6. Have access points been kept away from metal pillars, filing cabinets, ductwork or concrete walls, or other sources of interference (such as machinery) where possible?   ☐   ☐   ☐

Comments: _____

7. Have the appropriate access point antennae for the area been selected?   ☐   ☐   ☐

Comments: _____

8. Have the access points been placed to minimize cable distance from the telecommunications closets if possible?   ☐   ☐   ☐

Comments: _____

9. Is there an overlap of coverage between nodes? A 20 percent overlap in coverage for seamless roaming is a good rule of thumb.   ☐   ☐   ☐

Comments: _____

10. Is it possible to adjust node power to reduce or increase the signal to optimize the overlap instead of moving wireless access points physically closer or farther apart?   ☐   ☐   ☐

Comments: _____

F. Workstation Connections

1. What types of connections will be used in connecting the workstation equipment with the wired and/or wireless network? The work area components extend from the telecommunications outlet to each workstation.   ☐   ☐   ☐

Comments: _____

2. Is the work area wiring designed to be relatively simple to interconnect so that moves, new equipment, and changes are easily managed?   ☐   ☐   ☐

Comments: _____

3. Are there patch cables, modular cords, PC adapter cables, fiber jumpers, etc.?   ☐   ☐   ☐

Comments: _____

	YES	NO	N/A

4. Are adapters and baluns, etc., external to the telecommunications outlets?   ☐ ☐ ☐

Comments: _____

_____

G. Workstation Equipment

1. Do the workstations have

   a) Hidden wiring?   ☐ ☐ ☐

   b) All necessary connection outlets to link to the library's network?   ☐ ☐ ☐

   c) Adequate work space?   ☐ ☐ ☐

   d) Space for printers, paper, and supplies?   ☐ ☐ ☐

   e) Back panels to hide connections and wires from customers?   ☐ ☐ ☐

Comments: _____

_____

2. Will printers be available at every workstation, or will some or all workstations print to a network printer?   ☐ ☐ ☐

Comments: _____

_____

3. Are impact printers controlled?   ☐ ☐ ☐

Comments: _____

_____

4. Do electronic workstations provide applications for word processing, spreadsheets, media, communications, and other applications?   ☐ ☐ ☐

Comments: _____

_____

5. If there are not enough electronic workstations to meet peak demand, is there a system in place to allocate use?   ☐ ☐ ☐

Comments: _____

_____

H. Telephone System

1. Is there a central telephone system?   ☐ ☐ ☐

Comments: _____

_____

2. Does the telephone system provide for the following?

   a) An auto-attendant, the recorded message that answers your phones and instructs callers how to reach the person or department they are looking for   ☐ ☐ ☐

   b) Music-on-hold   ☐ ☐ ☐

	YES	NO	N/A
c) Voice mail	☐	☐	☐
d) Call forwarding	☐	☐	☐
e) Teleconferencing (audio or audio/video)	☐	☐	☐
f) Automatic redial	☐	☐	☐
g) Remote access	☐	☐	☐
h) Direct inward dialing	☐	☐	☐
i) Night service that puts the system into night mode	☐	☐	☐
j) Toll restriction on outgoing calls	☐	☐	☐
k) Paging	☐	☐	☐
l) Maintenance contract	☐	☐	☐
m) Future expansion capabilities	☐	☐	☐

Comments: _____

_____

3. Is a switchboard operator required?	☐	☐	☐

Comments: _____

_____

4. If so, is there adequate space for operators to do other work when not answering the phone?	☐	☐	☐

Comments: _____

_____

5. Are alternative long-distance vendors used?	☐	☐	☐

Comments: _____

_____

6. Are telephones hard-wired?	☐	☐	☐

Comments: _____

_____

7. Are incoming lines sufficient in number and quality?	☐	☐	☐

Comments: _____

_____

8. Are public telephones located to allow for convenient use while preventing disturbance to other customers?	☐	☐	☐

Comments: _____

_____

9. Are the public telephones set up for outgoing calls only?	☐	☐	☐

Comments: _____

_____

	YES	NO	N/A

10. Are telephone directories provided? ☐ ☐ ☐
Comments: _____
_____

11. Are coin-changing machines available near the telephones? ☐ ☐ ☐
Comments: _____
_____

12. Is the library involved in a network with branches, campus locations, and/or other libraries via telecommunications and data transfer? ☐ ☐ ☐
Comments: _____
_____

13. Will Voice-over-Internet Protocol (VoIP) be used? VoIP is a technology that allows users to make voice calls using a broadband Internet connection instead of a regular (or analog) phone line. Some VoIP services may allow calls only to other people using the same service, but others may allow calls to anyone who has a telephone number—including local, long distance, mobile, and international numbers. ☐ ☐ ☐
Comments: _____
_____

I. Miscellaneous Electrical Equipment

1. Are video monitors and television sets available for public use? ☐ ☐ ☐
Comments: _____
_____

2. Are audio players (DVD, MP3, etc.) available for use by the library's customers? ☐ ☐ ☐
Comments: _____
_____

3. Are the video sets controlled by staff? ☐ ☐ ☐
Comments: _____
_____

4. Is there provision for large-screen television viewing in meeting or conference rooms? ☐ ☐ ☐
Comments: _____
_____

5. Is there access to cable TV? ☐ ☐ ☐
Comments: _____
_____

6. Is there access to campus, private, government, or local broadcasts? ☐ ☐ ☐
Comments: _____
_____

		YES	NO	N/A
7.	Are there teleconferencing and distance-learning facilities?	☐	☐	☐
	Comments: _____			
	_____			
8.	Is microwave transmission/reception used?	☐	☐	☐
	Comments: _____			
	_____			
9.	Is there a public-address system?	☐	☐	☐
	Comments: _____			
	_____			
10.	Is there a video surveillance system?	☐	☐	☐
	Comments: _____			
	_____			

J. Electrical Power

		YES	NO	N/A
1.	Is there sufficient power distribution throughout the entire facility?	☐	☐	☐
	Comments: _____			
	_____			
2.	Is it "clean power," with high quality, and reliable?	☐	☐	☐
	Comments: _____			
	_____			
3.	Is there a backup power system in place?	☐	☐	☐
	Comments: _____			
	_____			
4.	Does the system provide for future needs?	☐	☐	☐
	Comments: _____			
	_____			
5.	Is all wiring easily accessible (raised floors, flat wire, grids under carpet, conduits above dropped ceilings or in columns)?	☐	☐	☐
	Comments: _____			
	_____			
6.	Is surge protection available where needed?	☐	☐	☐
	Comments: _____			
	_____			
7.	Is voltage regulated at the building feed?	☐	☐	☐
	Comments: _____			
	_____			

	YES	NO	N/A

8. Is voltage regulated at each floor box? ☐ ☐ ☐

Comments: _____

_____

9. Are dedicated lines available for equipment that requires them (terminals, photocopiers, etc.)? ☐ ☐ ☐

Comments: _____

_____

10. Are cords and cables protected and out of sight? ☐ ☐ ☐

Comments: _____

_____

11. Does each staff workstation have three to five duplex outlets? ☐ ☐ ☐

Comments: _____

_____

12. Are there convenience outlets at frequent intervals throughout the building? ☐ ☐ ☐

Comments: _____

_____

13. Do outlets have electrical and data/telephone capabilities? ☐ ☐ ☐

Comments: _____

_____

14. Are there specialized wiring arrangements (e.g., wall-mounted power strips or ceiling outlets) for areas such as teleconference, automated demonstration, and computing rooms? ☐ ☐ ☐

Comments: _____

_____

15. Are public workstations/carrels provided with power and data ports? ☐ ☐ ☐

Comments: _____

_____

16. Is there a user fee for using the library's power? ☐ ☐ ☐

Comments: _____

_____

8

Interior Design and Finishes

	YES	NO	N/A

A. Service Desks

1. Whom does the service desk serve (faculty, students, adults, children)? _____
   _____

   Comments: _____
   _____

2. What types of service desks are required?

	YES	NO	N/A
a) Control or security desk	☐	☐	☐
b) Directional or information desk	☐	☐	☐
c) Circulation or charge desk	☐	☐	☐
d) Children's desk	☐	☐	☐
e) Young adult desk	☐	☐	☐
f) Media center desk	☐	☐	☐
g) Call, reserve, or delivery desk	☐	☐	☐
h) Reference desk	☐	☐	☐
i) Reference or bibliographic consultation center	☐	☐	☐

   Comments: _____
   _____

3. Is the design of the desk area flexible, allowing possible future relocation, new
   technology, or even elimination of the desk? ☐ ☐ ☐

   Comments: _____
   _____

		YES	NO	N/A

4. What kinds of way-finding system and signs lead people to the service desks? _____

_____

Comments: _____

_____

5. Is the desk located in a visible location so that it is obvious to people who need the services provided at the desk? □ □ □

Comments: _____

_____

6. Is the desk sized to accommodate all staff working at the desk, as well as their storage requirements? □ □ □

Comments: _____

_____

7. Is the desk and surrounding work space designed to be ergonomically correct for staff and customers? □ □ □

Comments: _____

_____

8. Have customer self-service features been factored into the desk, such as self-checkout, electronic registration, etc.? □ □ □

Comments: _____

_____

9. Can conversations at the desk be conducted with a sense of privacy? □ □ □

Comments: _____

_____

10. How has noise from the service desk from conversations, equipment, phones, etc., been addressed so that nearby spaces are not disrupted? _____

_____

Comments: _____

_____

11. Have openness and accessibility been maintained while protecting staff from potentially aggressive customers? □ □ □

Comments: _____

_____

12. Are grommets, wire channels, and equipment shielding provided and designed to present a clean appearance? □ □ □

Comments: _____

_____

13. Have sufficient electrical outlets and data and telephone ports been provided for current use as well as anticipated use? □ □ □

Comments: _____

_____

	YES	NO	N/A

14. Is the desk protected from direct sunlight, drafts, or other adverse environmental conditions? ☐ ☐ ☐

Comments: _____

_____

15. Are the desk finishes and materials highly durable and relatively vandal proof? ☐ ☐ ☐

Comments: _____

_____

16. Can the desk surfaces and edges be easily cleaned? ☐ ☐ ☐

Comments: _____

_____

B. Seating

1. Is there variety in the types of seating? ☐ ☐ ☐

Comments: _____

_____

2. Is lounge seating modular or heavy enough to discourage casual rearrangement by customers, unless the library desires rearrangement? ☐ ☐ ☐

Comments: _____

_____

3. Is adequate and appropriate seating provided for the following tasks and areas?

   a) Staff work areas ☐ ☐ ☐

   b) Public seating at tables and carrels ☐ ☐ ☐

   c) Faculty and graduate carrels and rooms ☐ ☐ ☐

   d) Information commons ☐ ☐ ☐

   e) Reference areas ☐ ☐ ☐

   f) Lounge areas ☐ ☐ ☐

   g) Meeting rooms ☐ ☐ ☐

Comments: _____

_____

4. Is seating appropriate for different ages? ☐ ☐ ☐

Comments: _____

_____

5. Are people (especially senior citizens) able to get in and out of chairs easily? ☐ ☐ ☐

Comments: _____

_____

	YES	NO	N/A

6. Is seating comfortable for those areas where the library wants users to relax and read for an extended period? ☐ ☐ ☐

Comments: _____

_____

7. Is seating comfortable but conducive to quick turnover for those areas where you want users to leave after their work task is completed? (The two types of seating can be exemplified by the seating available in a fast-food restaurant versus that found in a fine-dining restaurant.) ☐ ☐ ☐

Comments: _____

_____

8. Are chairs ergonomically correct? ☐ ☐ ☐

Comments: _____

_____

9. Is seating attractive and inviting? ☐ ☐ ☐

Comments: _____

_____

10. Is furniture free of projections that could snag clothing? ☐ ☐ ☐

Comments: _____

_____

11. Is furniture relatively free from sharp corners? ☐ ☐ ☐

Comments: _____

_____

12. Does seating take personal space into consideration to avoid psychological feelings of crowding? ☐ ☐ ☐

Comments: _____

_____

13. If the chair has arms, will the arms fit comfortably under work surfaces? ☐ ☐ ☐

Comments: _____

_____

14. Are footstools or ottomans provided? ☐ ☐ ☐

Comments: _____

_____

15. Is furniture designed for easy repair or replacement of parts? ☐ ☐ ☐

Comments: _____

_____

16. Is furniture constructed for user safety? ☐ ☐ ☐

Comments: _____

_____

	YES	NO	N/A

17. Has the furniture been used successfully in similar library or other public situations for several years? ☐ ☐ ☐

Comments: _____

_____

18. Are performance data available to attest to the durability of the seating? ☐ ☐ ☐

Comments: _____

_____

19. Has the seating been stress tested? ☐ ☐ ☐

Comments: _____

_____

20. Have chairs been tested for at least one day by a variety of users? This test of "1,000 bottoms" should allow a variety (sex, height, weight) of people to sit in and use the furniture for at least one day. ☐ ☐ ☐

Comments: _____

_____

21. Do chairs with casters move easily on carpet? ☐ ☐ ☐

Comments: _____

_____

22. Is lounge seating modular or heavy enough not to tip over? ☐ ☐ ☐

Comments: _____

_____

23. Are fabrics sturdy and soil resistant? ☐ ☐ ☐

Comments: _____

_____

24. Do the chair design and the kind of upholstery or finish used allow for easy cleaning? ☐ ☐ ☐

Comments: _____

_____

25. Can the chair be easily reupholstered or refinished? ☐ ☐ ☐

Comments: _____

_____

26. Is the fabric porous enough to "breathe" and able to absorb and evaporate moisture easily? ☐ ☐ ☐

Comments: _____

_____

27. Do lounge chairs with upholstered arms have arm covers to preserve appearance? ☐ ☐ ☐

Comments: _____

_____

	YES	NO	N/A

28. Are chairs designed so that the area under the chair can be easily reached by a vacuum cleaner? ☐ ☐ ☐

 Comments: _____

 _____

29. Does the supplier warranty the design and construction of the seats? ☐ ☐ ☐

 Comments: _____

 _____

C. Tables

1. Are the tables appropriate for the task intended? ☐ ☐ ☐

 Comments: _____

 _____

2. Are the tables durable and strong? ☐ ☐ ☐

 Comments: _____

 _____

3. Is the work surface material appropriate for the use anticipated? ☐ ☐ ☐

 Comments: _____

 _____

4. Can the work surface be easily maintained? ☐ ☐ ☐

 Comments: _____

 _____

5. Can the work surface be easily refinished? ☐ ☐ ☐

 Comments: _____

 _____

6. Does the table have any needed accessories, such as task lighting, electrical outlets, etc.? ☐ ☐ ☐

 Comments: _____

 _____

7. Is there a mixture of circular tables (for socializing) and rectangular tables (better for work and concentration) on the floor? ☐ ☐ ☐

 Comments: _____

 _____

8. Are there enough carrels for individual studying? ☐ ☐ ☐

 Comments: _____

 _____

9. Does the supplier warranty the design and construction of the table? ☐ ☐ ☐

 Comments: _____

 _____

YES   NO   N/A

10. What is the length of the warranty? _____

    Comments: _____
    _____

D. Lighting

Please also see chapter 10 ("Building Systems"), section D, Lighting.

1. Is the intensity of the general lighting sufficient for reading?   ☐   ☐   ☐
   Comments: _____
   _____

2. Is the "task lighting" adequate for carrels, workstations, separate desks, lounge
   furniture, and shelving areas?   ☐   ☐   ☐
   Comments: _____
   _____

3. In addition to general and task lighting, do certain areas of the library have special
   lighting? For example, do wall display areas have track lighting?   ☐   ☐   ☐
   Comments: _____
   _____

4. Are the lights used to highlight display cases and exhibits nonglaring?   ☐   ☐   ☐
   Comments: _____
   _____

5. Is lighting adequate at the lower shelf areas in book stacks? (Lighting levels drop
   dramatically from the top to the bottom of book stacks.)   ☐   ☐   ☐
   Comments: _____
   _____

6. Are light switches conveniently located?   ☐   ☐   ☐
   Comments: _____
   _____

7. Can library staff control the switching of lights from a central control point
   or points?   ☐   ☐   ☐
   Comments: _____
   _____

8. Is the lighting control system designed so that customers can't switch lights on and
   off in those areas where public control is not desirable?   ☐   ☐   ☐
   Comments: _____
   _____

YES   NO   N/A

E. Windows

1. Has the library considered the trade-off between the positive aspects of operable windows (natural light, fresh air, and pleasant vistas) and the negative factors (the possible waste of energy, the loss of outside walls as book-stack areas, and the impact of uncontrolled sunlight on materials and readers)?   ☐   ☐   ☐

    Comments: _____
    _____

2. If the regional climate allows it, are windows operable to allow for natural cooling and ventilation?   ☐   ☐   ☐

    Comments: _____
    _____

3. If operable windows are used, how will staff control their use?   ☐   ☐   ☐
    Comments: _____
    _____

4. If windows can be opened, are they securable by the staff from the inside?   ☐   ☐   ☐
    Comments: _____
    _____

5. In those libraries where operable windows are not employed, are a limited number of windows operable to allow for maintenance and emergency situations?   ☐   ☐   ☐
    Comments: _____
    _____

6. Are some of the windows placed close to the ceiling to allow a higher intensity of light?   ☐   ☐   ☐
    Comments: _____
    _____

7. Are some of the windows placed at eye level, especially in reading areas and in areas occupied by the staff, for positive psychological effect?   ☐   ☐   ☐
    Comments: _____
    _____

8. Can windows be shaded on demand to prevent light from interfering with reading and other activities?   ☐   ☐   ☐
    Comments: _____
    _____

9. Are books stored away from direct sunlight to protect the bindings from fading and to prevent paper deterioration?   ☐   ☐   ☐
    Comments: _____
    _____

	YES	NO	N/A

10. If the regional climate suggests it, are windows double-glazed for enhanced energy efficiency? ☐ ☐ ☐

    Comments: _____

11. Are windows accessible for cleaning and maintenance? ☐ ☐ ☐

    Comments: _____

12. Will special equipment be required to maintain and clean windows? ☐ ☐ ☐

    Comments: _____

F. Flooring

1. Has the trade-off between types of floor coverings been considered by examining the following?

   a) Original construction costs ☐ ☐ ☐

   b) Total useful life of the floor covering ☐ ☐ ☐

   c) Appropriateness of the floor covering for the area to be covered (soiling potential, spills, noise, etc.) ☐ ☐ ☐

   d) Ease of maintenance ☐ ☐ ☐

   e) Cost of maintenance ☐ ☐ ☐

   f) Ease of replacement ☐ ☐ ☐

   g) Cost of replacement ☐ ☐ ☐

   Comments: _____

2. Are special floor-covering materials or systems used at the entry and places of heavy traffic to prevent dirt, mud, slush, and water from being tracked onto the carpet? ☐ ☐ ☐

   Comments: _____

3. Have carpet tiles or squares been considered for easy access to under-floor power systems as well as ease of replacement when damaged or soiled? ☐ ☐ ☐

   Comments: _____

4. Is the carpet of first-class quality to ensure durability? ☐ ☐ ☐

   Comments: _____

5. Does the carpet color conceal soiling and resist fading? ☐ ☐ ☐

   Comments: _____

	YES	NO	N/A
6. Does the flooring minimize noise and enhance building acoustics?	☐	☐	☐

Comments: _____

_____

	YES	NO	N/A
7. Can book trucks be moved easily across the flooring?	☐	☐	☐

Comments: _____

_____

| 8. Is ceramic tile or a similar material used on the restroom floors for its sanitary appearance and ease of maintenance? | ☐ | ☐ | ☐ |

Comments: _____

_____

| 9. If pavement tiles (stone, marble, or granite) are used in entryways and lobbies, are provisions made for safety since these have the potential to become very slippery when wet? | ☐ | ☐ | ☐ |

Comments: _____

_____

| 10. Has concrete flooring, if left uncovered, been treated with filler and then painted to prevent dust from becoming troublesome? | ☐ | ☐ | ☐ |

Comments: _____

_____

| 11. If wood floors are used, does the library's operating budget allow for the care needed to keep them in good condition? | ☐ | ☐ | ☐ |

Comments: _____

_____

G. Walls

| 1. Have "wet" interior walls been avoided as much as possible? (Wet walls are those that cannot be removed without demolishing them.) | ☐ | ☐ | ☐ |

Comments: _____

_____

| 2. Are the wall finishes, coverings, and surfaces appropriate for the room's function? | ☐ | ☐ | ☐ |

Comments: _____

_____

| 3. Will the care and selection of wall coverings result in years of added wear and minimum upkeep? | ☐ | ☐ | ☐ |

Comments: _____

_____

| 4. Are areas subject to soiling covered with a washable paint with a glossy finish? | ☐ | ☐ | ☐ |

Comments: _____

_____

	YES	NO	N/A
5. Is matte, or dull, finish used where reflectivity is a concern?	☐	☐	☐
Comments: _____			
6. To add interest, are there special wall treatments such as stenciling, textured materials such as a woven fabric, or wood paneling?	☐	☐	☐
Comments: _____			
7. Have other materials such as brick and stone been used for wall coverings?	☐	☐	☐
Comments: _____			
8. Is ceramic tile used for the walls in the restrooms for ease of maintenance?	☐	☐	☐
Comments: _____			
9. If ceramic tile has been used to create decorative wall murals, has care been taken to minimize the acoustical impact of the hard surface?	☐	☐	☐
Comments: _____			
10. Have vinyl wall coverings been considered for areas of heavy use, including hallways and staircases?	☐	☐	☐
Comments: _____			
11. Have vinyl wall coverings with special sound-absorbing properties been considered for offices, workrooms, and conference rooms?	☐	☐	☐
Comments: _____			
12. Do the walls have tackboard or other such surfaces so that they may be used for occasional displays?	☐	☐	☐
Comments: _____			

H. Color

	YES	NO	N/A
1. Have colors that may quickly become outdated been avoided?	☐	☐	☐
Comments: _____			
2. Has particular attention been given to the psychological effects of color on both users and staff?	☐	☐	☐
Comments: _____			

	YES	NO	N/A
3. Has color been considered with respect to the function of the area? Comments: _____	☐	☐	☐
4. Has color been used to avoid an institutional (drab) aspect with respect to walls, book stacks, floors, and furniture? Comments: _____	☐	☐	☐
5. Do book stacks on different floors or areas utilize different colors for easy identification? Comments: _____	☐	☐	☐
6. Have standard paint colors (not mixed) been supplied by the manufacturer for easy, cost-effective maintenance and touch-ups? Comments: _____	☐	☐	☐
7. Will the upholstery colors selected disguise heavy and sometimes abusive use? Comments: _____	☐	☐	☐

I. Equipment List

Is the following equipment planned for use in the library? If so, are adequate space, wiring, furniture, and staff available to support the equipment?

	YES	NO	N/A
1. Online public access terminals Comments: _____	☐	☐	☐
2. Public electronic workstations Comments: _____	☐	☐	☐
3. Public printers Comments: _____	☐	☐	☐
4. Staff telephones with hold and transfer capabilities Comments: _____	☐	☐	☐
5. Public telephones Comments: _____	☐	☐	☐

		YES	NO	N/A
6.	Mobile two-way communication system	☐	☐	☐
	Comments: _____			
7.	Answering machines or voice mail	☐	☐	☐
	Comments: _____			
8.	Staff paging communication devices	☐	☐	☐
	Comments: _____			
9.	Public-address system	☐	☐	☐
	Comments: _____			
10.	Telefacsimile (fax) machines	☐	☐	☐
	Comments: _____			
11.	Voice-synthesis reading machines	☐	☐	☐
	Comments: _____			
12.	Public text telephones (TDDs)	☐	☐	☐
	Comments: _____			
13.	Electric typewriters	☐	☐	☐
	Comments: _____			
14.	Large-print typewriters	☐	☐	☐
	Comments: _____			
15.	Word processor workstations	☐	☐	☐
	Comments: _____			
16.	Audio recorders/players	☐	☐	☐
	Comments: _____			
17.	Video recorders/players	☐	☐	☐
	Comments: _____			

	YES	NO	N/A
18. Tape duplicators	☐	☐	☐
Comments: _____			
_____			
19. MP3 players	☐	☐	☐
Comments: _____			
_____			
20. Video disc players	☐	☐	☐
Comments: _____			
_____			
21. Compact disc players	☐	☐	☐
Comments: _____			
_____			
22. Record players	☐	☐	☐
Comments: _____			
_____			
23. Audiocassette players	☐	☐	☐
Comments: _____			
_____			
24. Headphones	☐	☐	☐
Comments: _____			
_____			
25. Film projectors and screens	☐	☐	☐
Comments: _____			
_____			
26. Video projectors	☐	☐	☐
Comments: _____			
_____			
27. Slide projectors	☐	☐	☐
Comments: _____			
_____			
28. Light table (for viewing slides and/or tracing maps)	☐	☐	☐
Comments: _____			
_____			
29. Overhead projectors	☐	☐	☐
Comments: _____			
_____			

	YES	NO	N/A

30. Microform readers ☐ ☐ ☐
    Comments: _____
    _____

31. Microform readers/printers ☐ ☐ ☐
    Comments: _____
    _____

32. Photocopiers ☐ ☐ ☐
    Comments: _____
    _____

33. Card-operated photocopiers ☐ ☐ ☐
    Comments: _____
    _____

34. Clocks, strategically located and visible in all public places as well as easily
    accessible or centrally controlled ☐ ☐ ☐
    Comments: _____
    _____

35. Time clocks ☐ ☐ ☐
    Comments: _____
    _____

36. Fire hoses ☐ ☐ ☐
    Comments: _____
    _____

37. Fire extinguishers ☐ ☐ ☐
    Comments: _____
    _____

38. Emergency lights ☐ ☐ ☐
    Comments: _____
    _____

39. Emergency power (generators) ☐ ☐ ☐
    Comments: _____
    _____

40. Closed-circuit TV systems ☐ ☐ ☐
    Comments: _____
    _____

41. Security mirrors ☐ ☐ ☐
    Comments: _____
    _____

	YES	NO	N/A
42. Emergency call system directly to police or security company	☐	☐	☐
Comments: _____			
43. Emergency call buttons located at service desks and in workrooms	☐	☐	☐
Comments: _____			
44. Book trucks:			
a) Are they top quality with solid joints and pivoting wheels?	☐	☐	☐
b) Do they roll smoothly and quietly on all floor surfaces?	☐	☐	☐
c) Are they equipped with shelf height, depth, and slant to accommodate materials of various sizes?	☐	☐	☐
d) Are there sufficient quantities of trucks in various sizes and configurations?	☐	☐	☐
Comments: _____			
45. Chalkboards/white boards	☐	☐	☐
Comments: _____			
46. Bulletin boards	☐	☐	☐
Comments: _____			
47. Easels	☐	☐	☐
Comments: _____			
48. Lecterns	☐	☐	☐
Comments: _____			
49. Display racks	☐	☐	☐
Comments: _____			
50. Marketing fixtures	☐	☐	☐
Comments: _____			
51. Bookends in appropriate sizes and shapes	☐	☐	☐
Comments: _____			
52. Pencil sharpeners	☐	☐	☐
Comments: _____			

	YES	NO	N/A
53. Pencil dispensers	☐	☐	☐
Comments: _____			
54. Customer vending machines for supplies	☐	☐	☐
Comments: _____			
55. Filing cabinets	☐	☐	☐
Comments: _____			
56. Electric staplers	☐	☐	☐
Comments: _____			
57. Hole punches	☐	☐	☐
Comments: _____			
58. Paper cutters	☐	☐	☐
Comments: _____			
59. Board cutter	☐	☐	☐
Comments: _____			
60. Wire stitching machine	☐	☐	☐
Comments: _____			
61. Label-pasting machine	☐	☐	☐
Comments: _____			
62. Standing press	☐	☐	☐
Comments: _____			
63. Laminating machine	☐	☐	☐
Comments: _____			
64. Sign and label makers	☐	☐	☐
Comments: _____			

	YES	NO	N/A
65. Vacuum cleaners	☐	☐	☐
Comments: _____			
66. Cleaning supplies and supply carts	☐	☐	☐
Comments: _____			
67. Mops, buckets, brooms, and dustpans	☐	☐	☐
Comments: _____			
68. Trash compactor	☐	☐	☐
Comments: _____			
69. Wastebaskets	☐	☐	☐
Comments: _____			
70. Recycling containers	☐	☐	☐
Comments: _____			
71. Short and tall ladders and scaffolds	☐	☐	☐
Comments: _____			
72. Step stools	☐	☐	☐
Comments: _____			
73. Moving equipment (dollies, carts)	☐	☐	☐
Comments: _____			
74. Storage crates?	☐	☐	☐
Comments: _____			

J. Behavioral Aspects of Space

1. Has the library's desired atmosphere been considered in planning the building?
   Atmosphere is the conscious designing of space to create certain effects in users.
   It represents the interface between the user or customer and the organization.
   It is a relationship of feelings; it is a rapport with the user.   ☐   ☐   ☐

   Comments: _____

	YES	NO	N/A

2. Have the following external atmospheric elements been considered?

    a) Architecture ☐ ☐ ☐

    b) Visibility ☐ ☐ ☐

    c) Entrances ☐ ☐ ☐

    d) Display windows ☐ ☐ ☐

    e) Surrounding area ☐ ☐ ☐

    f) Congestion around the building ☐ ☐ ☐

    Comments: _____

3. Have the following internal atmospheric elements been considered?

    a) Colors ☐ ☐ ☐

    b) Lighting ☐ ☐ ☐

    c) Scents and sounds ☐ ☐ ☐

    d) Furniture and fixtures ☐ ☐ ☐

    e) Flooring ☐ ☐ ☐

    f) Temperature and humidity ☐ ☐ ☐

    g) Graphics ☐ ☐ ☐

    h) Aisle width ☐ ☐ ☐

    i) Vertical transportation ☐ ☐ ☐

    j) Service desk placement ☐ ☐ ☐

    k) Interior displays ☐ ☐ ☐

    l) Wall textures ☐ ☐ ☐

    Comments: _____

4. Does arriving at the library create a favorable impression in the minds of customers? This impression, or atmospherics, is created through elements such as store lighting, temperature, noise level, scents, wall coverings, architecture, and display fixtures that can be manipulated by retailers to produce an effect on consumers' buying habits. Atmospherics are thought to influence the customer's shopping moods and time spent in the store and are used to create or reinforce the customer's desire to buy a product. Think about how an Apple or Nike retail store creates excitement by its design and try to match that in the library building. ☐ ☐ ☐

    Comments: _____

5. Is there change in the library that will attract users? Window spaces and outdoor displays may encourage use of the library. ☐ ☐ ☐

    Comments: _____

	YES	NO	N/A

6. Has the library space been designed to optimize customer service? Customer service is the experience that library users have in interacting with library staff, collections, and facilities (electronically as well as in a physical building). ☐   ☐   ☐

Comments: _____

_____

7. In designing the library, have the following factors been considered in establishing how library customer service will be delivered:

a) Have all the physical and electronic points where customers experience service in the library been charted? These are customer "encounter points" or service points, and they help create an opinion of the library by its customers. ☐   ☐   ☐

b) Have standards been set for all service points (for example, time from initial request for materials in an Automated Storage and Retrieval System, or ASRS, to delivery at the circulation desk is less than ten minutes)? ☐   ☐   ☐

c) Have standards been communicated to library customers? ☐   ☐   ☐

d) Has staff been trained on building and maintaining a good relationship with customers? ☐   ☐   ☐

e) Is ongoing service monitored to ensure that standards are met? If you can't measure it, you can't manage it. ☐   ☐   ☐

Comments: _____

_____

8. Has space been designed to meet the unique needs of different segments of customers? Some examples are faculty, students, children, seniors, and young adults. Each segment may have different design needs. ☐   ☐   ☐

Comments: _____

_____

9. When designing library spaces, consider the following (based partially on Joseph Pine and James Gilmore's *The Experience Economy*).

a) What can be done to improve the aesthetics of the experience for customers? This is the quality that makes your customers want to come in to the library and spend time in the library, and it is achieved by making the environment more inviting, interesting, and comfortable. _____

_____

_____

b) What experiences do you want your customers to have in the library, and how will the space be designed to enhance their ability to have these experiences? Do you want customers to take out books, study, attend programs, use the information commons, and more? You probably envision a combination of activities, and spaces should be designed to accommodate each activity. _____

_____

_____

c) What do you want your customers to learn from experiencing the library space? How will you encourage them to explore and gain knowledge and experience? _____

_____

_____

| | YES | NO | N/A |

d) How can you make the library experience enjoyable for customers and encourage them to be repeat customers? What can be done to make the library an entertaining experience? _____

_____

_____

Comments: _____

_____

10. Has the following design thinking been used in designing the library space (based partially on "Design Thinking" by Steven J. Bell):

	YES	NO	N/A
a) Do you understand the physical library needs of your target customer population?	☐	☐	☐
b) Do you understand how your customers view your library's products, services, and facilities?	☐	☐	☐
c) Have you used marketing research to define what your customers want from their library services?	☐	☐	☐
d) Have you undertaken "anthropological research" by observing what your customer base does in the library?	☐	☐	☐
e) Have you used all the information you gathered to help define the physical library needs of your building?	☐	☐	☐

Comments: _____

_____

11. Have the following feng shui principles been considered in designing the library:

	YES	NO	N/A
a) Does the space meet the three C's of feng shui: clean, clear, and comfortable?	☐	☐	☐
b) Have the basic principles of the five natural elements (earth, water, fire, metal, and wood) been placed around the library and balanced to increase the flow of chi, or energy? Elements can be balanced internally using interior design and externally with landscape design. An object's element is determined by its color, shape, and material (e.g., the reflective nature of glass windows makes them a water element). Color, texture, and shape often determine the element.	☐	☐	☐

c) Is the library site square or rectangular? _____

_____

	YES	NO	N/A
d) Does it have a water view?	☐	☐	☐
e) Is the main entrance unblocked and easily visible when approaching the building?	☐	☐	☐
f) Does the building have only one main entrance? (This is a good feature no matter what design principles are used.)	☐	☐	☐
g) Has a straight-run stairway been avoided close to the main entry? A U-shaped or split stairway at right angles to the front entry is preferable.	☐	☐	☐
h) Have both yin and yang spaces been used? A space that is considered yang has high ceilings, expansive views, bright colors, or intense lighting. A space that is considered yin would have low ceilings, minimal openings, dark colors, or low lighting. Most libraries are yang in their public spaces.	☐	☐	☐

	YES	NO	N/A

i) Has a feng shui consultant been retained? A consultant can help the architect
and interior designer make the library space more attractive and improve staff
and customer well-being.   ☐   ☐   ☐

Comments: _____

_____

12. With access to electronic resources available to customers from their homes, what is the library doing to encourage
traveling to the library? How can a trip to the library be an experience? _____

_____

Comments: _____

_____

9

Materials Handling and Storage: Book Stacks and Shelving

	YES	NO	N/A

A. Conventional Stationary Stacks and Shelving

1. Has sufficient shelving been planned to meet the current and future needs of the library? (Consider the size of the current collection, the growth of the collection for at least twenty years, and the percentage of the collection that will be out on loan. A rule of thumb for roughly calculating shelving requirements is to assume 150 volumes per 3-foot single-faced section, seven shelves high.) ☐ ☐ ☐

   Comments: _____

2. Is the shelving selection based on the American National Standard for Single-Tier Steel Bracket Library Shelving, ANSI/NISO Z39.73-1994? This is the standard for shelving. ☐ ☐ ☐

   Comments: _____

3. Are book stacks arranged sequentially in parallel ranges so that users can easily locate materials? ☐ ☐ ☐

   Comments: _____

4. If book stacks are not arranged sequentially in parallel ranges, are variations clearly indicated? ☐ ☐ ☐

   Comments: _____

	YES	NO	N/A

5. Are there labels on both ends of ranges? ☐ ☐ ☐

Comments: _____

_____

6. Is display shelving included to merchandise the collection? For example, are there

   a) Display units with sloping shelves? ☐ ☐ ☐

   b) Point-of-purchase displays as seen in bookstores and department stores? ☐ ☐ ☐

   c) Spinners or towers? ☐ ☐ ☐

   d) Slatwall end panels or wall units? ☐ ☐ ☐

Comments: _____

_____

7. Are all stacks and shelves clearly labeled as to content on both end panels and shelf lips? ☐ ☐ ☐

Comments: _____

_____

8. Are there attempts to break the monotony of shelving by creative arrangement of seating or height and/or type of shelving? ☐ ☐ ☐

Comments: _____

_____

9. Are there no more than eight 36-inch shelving sections without a break? ☐ ☐ ☐

Comments: _____

_____

10. Have length of shelving and width of aisles been determined on the basis of traffic patterns and user accessibility? (See the ADA guidelines throughout chapter 6.) ☐ ☐ ☐

Comments: _____

_____

11. Are the shelving height and depth adequate for users? ☐ ☐ ☐

Comments: _____

_____

12. Do single-faced sections of bracket shelving have bases 20 inches deep? ☐ ☐ ☐

   Do double-faced sections of bracket shelving have bases 40 inches deep? ☐ ☐ ☐

Comments: _____

_____

13. Is freestanding shelving, ranging from 78 inches and higher, anchored to the floor, braced with top tie struts, or both? _____

Comments: _____

_____

14. Are the shelving units

   a) Sturdy and well built? ☐ ☐ ☐

   b) Able to bear prescribed loads without sagging, bending, leaning, swaying, or collapsing? ☐ ☐ ☐

	YES	NO	N/A
c) Equipped with a finish that will endure normal use and cleaning for at least thirty years without signs of wear?	☐	☐	☐
d) Smoothly finished with no burrs or sharp edges?	☐	☐	☐
e) Standardized in design and color?	☐	☐	☐
f) Designed to have interchangeable parts?	☐	☐	☐
g) Equipped with adjustable shelves?	☐	☐	☐
h) Equipped with shelves that are relatively easy to move when they are nloaded?	☐	☐	☐
i) Equipped with shelves that are relatively easy to move when they are loaded?	☐	☐	☐
j) Braced and/or anchored to comply with local regulations?	☐	☐	☐
k) Equipped with end panels?	☐	☐	☐
l) Equipped with canopies?	☐	☐	☐

Comments: _____

15. Are there special features such as the following?

	YES	NO	N/A
a) Pullout shelves	☐	☐	☐
b) Built-in lighting	☐	☐	☐
c) Electrical access	☐	☐	☐
d) Shelf dividers	☐	☐	☐
e) Movable book supports of adequate size	☐	☐	☐
f) Range-label holders	☐	☐	☐
g) Shelf-label holders	☐	☐	☐
h) Current periodical shelves	☐	☐	☐
i) Wide-lip newspaper shelves	☐	☐	☐
j) Atlas and dictionary stands	☐	☐	☐

Comments: _____

16. Are there accessories to display and house the following?

	YES	NO	N/A
a) CDs	☐	☐	☐
b) DVDs	☐	☐	☐
c) Audiocassettes	☐	☐	☐
d) Videocassettes	☐	☐	☐
e) Picture books	☐	☐	☐
f) Paperback books	☐	☐	☐
g) Oversized and miniature materials	☐	☐	☐
h) Archival materials	☐	☐	☐
i) Films, filmstrips, slides, microforms	☐	☐	☐
j) Realia	☐	☐	☐
k) Other odd-shaped items	☐	☐	☐

Comments: _____

	YES	NO	N/A

17. Does periodical shelving have a maximum reach height of 48 inches? ☐ ☐ ☐

Comments: _____

_____

18. Does periodical shelving have sloping shelves that tilt and allow for storage on a flat shelf beneath? ☐ ☐ ☐

Comments: _____

_____

19. Is the edge or lip on newspaper shelves wide enough to hold a large Sunday edition? (Use the *New York Times* for the Sunday after Thanksgiving as a test.) ☐ ☐ ☐

Comments: _____

_____

20. Is there a need for enclosed shelving with lockable doors? ☐ ☐ ☐

Comments: _____

_____

21. Are there shelf/table units for reference and index materials? ☐ ☐ ☐

Comments: _____

_____

22. Have nonpublic work and storage areas been provided with appropriate shelving? ☐ ☐ ☐

Comments: _____

_____

23. Have the following aisle allowances been made:

   a) Are cross aisles that run parallel to the stack aisles and that are intended to break up the stack aisles into increments (also known as range aisles) a minimum of 36 inches wide to meet accessibility requirements? (Some libraries prefer 42 to 48 inches.) ☐ ☐ ☐

   b) Are end aisles that run perpendicular to stack aisles and may have books on one side a minimum of 36 inches wide? (In some cases, 44 inches is required.) ☐ ☐ ☐

   c) Are main aisles a minimum of 44 inches wide? These aisles serve as the principal accessible routes. ☐ ☐ ☐

Comments: _____

_____

B. Movable-Aisle Compact Shelving

1. Is there a need for movable-aisle compact shelving? These are shelving systems that ride on movable carriages over floor-installed rails. This shelving maximizes use of floor space by having only one access aisle, which is located by moving the carriage-mounted shelving to the desired location for the aisle opening. ☐ ☐ ☐

Comments: _____

_____

	YES	NO	N/A

2. If the rails cannot be recessed, will there be some kind of deck for the system?   ☐ ☐ ☐

   Comments: _____

   _____

3. Is the building capable of holding the substantial weight of a compact installation? (Generally, floor load capacity for compact shelving is 300 pounds live load per square foot, or double the amount required for conventional shelving.)   ☐ ☐ ☐

   Comments: _____

   _____

4. Does the cost of the space saved justify the cost of the system?   ☐ ☐ ☐

   Comments: _____

   _____

5. Are all ADA and safety codes met?   ☐ ☐ ☐

   Comments: _____

   _____

6. What type of system is being considered? _____

   _____

   - A manual system operates with a push or pull of the handle to move the shelving units stored on carriages that move from side to side. Shelving systems can range from two to four sections of shelving deep. Sections of shelving are easily moved to the side, exposing another section of shelving behind the original layer. Human power is strained after the number of sections exceeds four.
   - A mechanical assistance system moves the stacks with a turn of a handle attached to a pulley or a lever at the end of the stack range that is connected to a gear system that drives the range. Mechanical Assistance Mobile Shelving systems require only the turn of a handle to access shelves. Usually 1 pound of pressure can move thousands of pounds of steel and media.
   - An electrical system moves the stacks by pushing a button on a control panel activating one or more electrical motors. Some systems may be configured with multiple aisles without compromising safety. There usually is a system indicator light that alerts users of the unit's operational status. The control panel may be located to meet ADA requirements.

   Comments: _____

   _____

7. If an electrical system is used, does it have a manual override?   ☐ ☐ ☐

   Comments: _____

   _____

8. Does the electrical system have

   a) An emergency stop button?   ☐ ☐ ☐

   b) An automatic lock after displacement?   ☐ ☐ ☐

   c) Protection against radio frequency interferences?   ☐ ☐ ☐

   d) A toe-level infrared beam to detect people in the stacks?   ☐ ☐ ☐

   Comments: _____

   _____

	YES	NO	N/A

9. Is there a "fail-safe system" that stops the movement of the units if an obstacle (especially a person) is encountered?   ☐   ☐   ☐

   Comments: _____

   _____

10. Have the specialized cleaning and maintenance needs of compact shelving been considered? ☐   ☐   ☐

    Comments: _____

    _____

11. Under the purchase agreement, how long will the vendor maintain the system? _____

    _____

    Comments: _____

    _____

12. Will movable stacks be accessible to the public with or without staff assistance? _____

    _____

    Comments: _____

    _____

13. If the movable stacks are not accessible to the public without staff assistance, what sorts of devices will be employed to keep the movable stacks from operating? _____

    _____

    Comments: _____

    _____

14. Can the system be expanded?   ☐   ☐   ☐

    Comments: _____

    _____

15. Can the system be moved easily to another location?   ☐   ☐   ☐

    Comments: _____

    _____

C. Automated Storage and Retrieval System (ASRS)

1. Is a mechanized book-retrieval system (ASRS) needed? To determine if an ASRS is justified, a cost-benefit analysis should be done measuring the floor space that will be gained (or not built) against the cost of the system and the potential inconvenience to users. An ASRS typically works as follows: ☐   ☐   ☐

   • Books and media are stored in bins on a rack structure. The bins are arranged by aisles, each of which has a "mini-load crane" guided by rails at top and bottom.

   • Books and media are stored in bins in the ASRS by bar code or RFID tag.

   • Requests for retrieval of ASRS items are submitted via the library catalog and are transmitted electronically to a designated circulation desk.

   • The request triggers the ASRS automatic crane in the appropriate aisle to deliver the bin to a designated pickup station.

   Comments: _____

   _____

	YES	NO	N/A

2. Have the following been considered before deciding upon a mechanized book-retrieval system?

   a) Size of the collection □ □ □

   b) Space available for the collection □ □ □

   c) Annual growth of the collection □ □ □

   d) Policy as to what will be stored in the ASRS □ □ □

   e) Policy on how long customers will have to wait for a book after it is requested from the ASRS □ □ □

   f) Cost of staffing the ASRS and the circulation desk □ □ □

   g) Cost of installation and maintenance □ □ □

   h) Load-bearing capabilities of the building □ □ □

   i) Contingency plans if the ASRS fails □ □ □

Comments: _____

3. Will installation of the system require any organizational changes that may impact the physical library building? □ □ □

Comments: _____

D. Materials Handling Systems

1. Has a materials handling system been considered? This is a self-service return and sorting system that automates material handling tasks such as sorting and returning materials to the shelves. These systems employ RFID tags for material handling. □ □ □

Comments: _____

2. Does the system provide the following services?

   a) *Automated check-in and sorting.* When a book, CD, or other item is returned to the library, it drops onto an automated conveyor system that carries materials to a sorting area. The book is actually checked back in to the library's circulation system by radio frequency identification (RFID) technology—an RFID antenna detects an RFID chip on the returned book. □ □ □

   b) *Automated routing and sorting within the library.* If the materials will stay at the library where they are returned, they are routed to sorting machines that place items on book carts for re-shelving. □ □ □

   c) *Automated routing and sorting to another library.* If the materials are directed to another library, they are routed to a series of motorized bins for delivery to another location. These bins have movable floors that raise or lower as items are added or removed. This feature prevents staff from having to bend and reach deep into the bin to remove items from the bottom. □ □ □

Comments: _____

	YES	NO	N/A

3. Do the elements of the system consist of the following?

    a) Automated check-in   ☐ ☐ ☐

    b) Automated checkout   ☐ ☐ ☐

    c) Reserve pickup   ☐ ☐ ☐

    d) Circulation materials sorting   ☐ ☐ ☐

    e) Patron reserve retrieval and storage systems   ☐ ☐ ☐

    f) Conveyor lift units   ☐ ☐ ☐

    g) RFID tracking   ☐ ☐ ☐

    h) Circulation materials conveying systems   ☐ ☐ ☐

    Comments: _____

_____

4. Does the system provide the following benefits?

    a) Reduces the time it takes to get books and other materials back in circulation after they've been returned   ☐ ☐ ☐

    b) Reduces the risk of personal injury to library staff caused by the repetitive motion and physical strain involved in sorting and moving books on a regular basis   ☐ ☐ ☐

    c) Allows self-checkout. This is usually faster than interacting with staff, especially if a number of materials are being checked out at the same time.   ☐ ☐ ☐

    d) Provides greater security and inventory control through RFID. This technology usually enhances materials security, reducing theft and associated costs.   ☐ ☐ ☐

    Comments: _____

_____

E. Remote Storage

1. Has an off-site storage facility been considered as a place to house secondary or little-used materials?   ☐ ☐ ☐

    Comments: _____

_____

2. Has a policy been established determining what will be placed in remote storage and what will remain in the library?   ☐ ☐ ☐

    Comments: _____

_____

3. Will the remote storage facility serve one library or will it store books cooperatively from a number of libraries?

_____

_____

    Comments: _____

_____

	YES	NO	N/A

4. If the facility will serve as a cooperative storage facility, have policies been negotiated to meet the needs of all members of the cooperative? ☐ ☐ ☐

Comments: _____

_____

5. Is the facility a cold-storage warehouse that maximizes the use of space through high-density shelving? ☐ ☐ ☐

Comments: _____

_____

6. Has a policy decision been made to store materials by size or by subject classifications? ☐ ☐ ☐

Comments: _____

_____

7. Does the remote storage facility have a high degree of book storage density, narrow aisles, long ranges of shelving, and shelving by size divisions in order to approach maximum density? Size versus subject is usually the standard policy. ☐ ☐ ☐

Comments: _____

_____

8. Will compact shelving units be used? ☐ ☐ ☐

Comments: _____

_____

9. Is the off-site storage facility designed to environmentally protect materials?

   a) Is the facility insulated and does it have a high degree of air tightness and vapor barriers compared to standard construction? Usually this means twice the insulation value and six times the air tightness, and a vapor barrier that is fifteen times that of standard construction. ☐ ☐ ☐

   b) Does the HVAC&R system provide an environment of approximately 55 to 65 degrees Fahrenheit and 40 to 55 percent relative humidity regardless of seasonal changes? ☐ ☐ ☐

   c) Is the HVAC&R system designed to quickly react to changes in the exterior climate? ☐ ☐ ☐

Comments: _____

_____

10. Is low lighting (sodium vapor or fluorescent light fixtures with UV shields) used in order to reduce the damage that light does to books? ☐ ☐ ☐

Comments: _____

_____

11. Is the amount of time that lights are left on kept to a minimum? ☐ ☐ ☐

Comments: _____

_____

12. Is public access available at the site for faculty, students, library users, etc? ☐ ☐ ☐

Comments: _____

_____

	YES	NO	N/A

13. If access is available, may customers browse the facility or only read?_____

_____

Comments: _____

_____

14. Is there space for processing in the facility?   ☐   ☐   ☐
Comments: _____

_____

15. Is there a high-security area for special collections?   ☐   ☐   ☐
Comments: _____

_____

16. Is the location of stored materials linked through barcodes, RFID tags, or
inventory control numbers to the library's catalog?   ☐   ☐   ☐
Comments: _____

_____

17. If stored materials are not linked to the library's catalog, is there an inventory
control system used at the storage facility to easily locate and retrieve materials? ☐   ☐   ☐
Comments: _____

_____

18. Has a delivery system been established for quick access to the stored collections
for library customers?   ☐   ☐   ☐
Comments: _____

_____

19. Have customer service standards been established for time to retrieve materials
from remote storage back to the library?   ☐   ☐   ☐
Comments: _____

_____

20. Has an electronic document system been established to enhance on-site access of
remote collections and reduce the number of materials that will need to be stored
off-site?   ☐   ☐   ☐
Comments: _____

_____

10

Building Systems

	YES	NO	N/A

A. Acoustics

1. Is an acoustic engineer part of the architect's design team? ☐ ☐ ☐

   Comments: _____

2. Has the ambient noise level been considered in siting the library building? ☐ ☐ ☐

   Comments: _____

3. If the selected site is noisy, has the building been positioned to mitigate ambient noise as much as possible? ☐ ☐ ☐

   Comments: _____

4. How does the library deal with noise?

   a) Does the library want noise control? With noise control, the library typically seeks to block noise through barriers masking the noise from equipment, facilities, and the surroundings. ☐ ☐ ☐

   b) Does the library want soundproofing? With soundproofing, the library is typically seeking to absorb sound or deal with echo and reverberation problems. ☐ ☐ ☐

   Comments: _____

	YES	NO	N/A

5. Is the library too quiet? If it is too quiet, the slightest sounds may distract users. ☐ ☐ ☐

Comments: _____

_____

6. Are circulation, information, and reference service points located and designed so noise will not disrupt other areas? ☐ ☐ ☐

Comments: _____

_____

7. Have restrooms, conference rooms, lounges, photocopiers, and public telephones been located where the noise will be the least distracting? ☐ ☐ ☐

Comments: _____

_____

8. Have the following elements been chosen to contribute to noise reduction?

   a) Carpeting ☐ ☐ ☐

   b) Other floor surfaces that do not generate and/or transfer noise ☐ ☐ ☐

   c) Wall coverings ☐ ☐ ☐

   d) Window coverings ☐ ☐ ☐

   e) Ceiling surfaces ☐ ☐ ☐

   f) Furniture ☐ ☐ ☐

   g) Shelving ☐ ☐ ☐

   h) Equipment ☐ ☐ ☐

Comments: _____

_____

9. Have quiet-opening doors and windows been selected? ☐ ☐ ☐

Comments: _____

_____

10. Has equipment in public areas (computer printers, photocopiers, etc.) been chosen for quiet operation? ☐ ☐ ☐

Comments: _____

_____

11. Has a sound masking system been considered? A sound masking system renders noise and conversation more difficult—or impossible—to comprehend. It also reduces dynamic range (the variation in sound over time), making a space feel quieter. ☐ ☐ ☐

Comments: _____

_____

12. Is there background sound, such as the ventilating system or other "white noise" sources, to mask minor distracting sounds? ☐ ☐ ☐

Comments: _____

_____

	YES	NO	N/A

13. What sound levels are desired for the library? _____
_____

Sound levels are measured in units of decibels (dB). Suggested sound levels are as follows:

- Quiet reading rooms: 30 dB
- Open reading areas: 45 dB
- Areas where normal conversation takes place: 60–70 dB
- Circulation desks, workrooms: 60–75 dB

Comments: _____
_____

14. If the exterior environment of the library has a high noise level, has location and type of window been considered in planning fenestration? ☐ ☐ ☐
Comments: _____
_____

15. Are traffic patterns throughout the building designed to keep noise and confusion away from readers? ☐ ☐ ☐
Comments: _____
_____

16. Are there acoustically controlled quiet areas, and are they accessible from widely distributed entrance points? ☐ ☐ ☐
Comments: _____
_____

17. Are soundproof rooms available? ☐ ☐ ☐
Comments: _____
_____

18. Are there areas where furniture is arranged so as to discourage conversation? ☐ ☐ ☐
Comments: _____
_____

19. In order to control noise levels in public rooms, have
   a) Walls been extended from floor to structural deck above? ☐ ☐ ☐
   b) Ceiling tiles been selected that have a good sound insulation quality? ☐ ☐ ☐
   c) Air ducts been balanced to reduce air noise? ☐ ☐ ☐
   d) Mechanical equipment rooms not been located close to public or staff areas? ☐ ☐ ☐
Comments: _____
_____

20. Is there acoustical separation between public and staff areas? ☐ ☐ ☐
Comments: _____
_____

	YES	NO	N/A

21. Have suspended ceilings with noise absorbing materials been considered? □ □ □

Comments: _____

_____

22. Have HVAC&R systems been specified to have an ambient sound level compatible with the occupancy? If the HVAC&R system is too noisy, conversation may be difficult. If the HVAC&R system is too quiet, unwanted conversations and other distracting noises will be heard. Usually quieter systems cost more but in the long run are worth it. □ □ □

Comments: _____

_____

23. Are mechanical systems (elevators, heating and air-conditioning equipment) located away from quiet areas and/or acoustically shielded? □ □ □

Comments: _____

_____

24. Have noisy equipment and activities been located where the sound may be dampened or have they been located in remote areas? □ □ □

Comments: _____

_____

B. Heating, Ventilating, Air-Conditioning, and Refrigerating (HVAC&R) Systems

1. Have all the following main functions of an HVAC&R system been considered?

   a) Heating that maintains adequate room temperature especially during colder weather conditions □ □ □

   b) Ventilation, which is associated with air movement. Adequate ventilation allows carbon dioxide to go out and oxygen to get in, allowing library users to inhale fresh air. □ □ □

   c) Air-conditioning system that controls temperature as well as ventilation □ □ □

   d) Humidity control. This is especially important in libraries because of the paper and other media housed in the building. This includes both humidification (adding moisture to the building) and dehumidification (reducing moisture in the building). □ □ □

   Comments: _____

   _____

2. Is the HVAC&R system

   a) Simple to operate? □ □ □

   b) Easy to maintain? □ □ □

   c) Efficient to run? □ □ □

   Comments: _____

   _____

		YES	NO	N/A

3. Does the system, including ductwork, make efficient use of space? ☐ ☐ ☐

Comments: _____

_____

4. Can temperature and humidity be zone-controlled room by room, either centrally or from lockable thermostats? ☐ ☐ ☐

Comments: _____

_____

5. Is there a remote system of control such as BACnet? ☐ ☐ ☐

- BACnet is a data communication protocol for building automation and nontrol networks. It was developed under the auspices of the American Society of Heating, Refrigerating and Air-Conditioning Engineers (ASHRAE). BACnet is an American national standard, a European standard, and a national standard in more than thirty countries, as well as an ISO global standard.

- A BACnet system can control

     HVAC&R systems

     Fire detection and alarm

     Lighting

     Security

     Smart elevators

     Utility company interface

- The system allows monitoring of building systems as well as adjustments of the systems from remote locations.

Comments: _____

_____

6. Is the building properly insulated to help maintain temperature efficiently? ☐ ☐ ☐

Comments: _____

_____

7. If the building has large windows or skylights, is there provision for maintaining temperature through window coverings or special glazing? ☐ ☐ ☐

Comments: _____

_____

8. Is there adequate ventilation using

   a) A mechanical air-exchange system? ☐ ☐ ☐

   b) Natural ventilation? ☐ ☐ ☐

Comments: _____

_____

9. Is there provision for ventilation if the climate control fails? ☐ ☐ ☐

Comments: _____

_____

	YES	NO	N/A

10. Do the windows open? ☐ ☐ ☐

If so, is this controlled by staff? ☐ ☐ ☐

Comments: _____

_____

11. Can environmental pollution be filtered out of the air? ☐ ☐ ☐

Comments: _____

_____

12. Can relative humidity (RH) be controlled for various types of media within a 5 percent variance?

a) *Books and paper:* 40 to 55 percent RH ☐ ☐ ☐

b) *Books, papers, and photos:* 50 percent RH ☐ ☐ ☐

c) *Magnetic media:* 30 percent RH ☐ ☐ ☐

Comments: _____

_____

13. Are temperature/humidity conditions appropriate for the following?

a) Rare materials ☐ ☐ ☐

b) Special collections ☐ ☐ ☐

c) Archives ☐ ☐ ☐

d) Electronic workstations, information commons, and telecommunications rooms ☐ ☐ ☐

e) Public areas ☐ ☐ ☐

f) Staff work areas ☐ ☐ ☐

g) Closed stacks ☐ ☐ ☐

Comments: _____

_____

14. Are there emergency backup generators that can be used if the electricity goes off
and the air-conditioning shuts down? ☐ ☐ ☐

Comments: _____

_____

C. Electrical Systems

1. Has the electrical system been planned for flexibility using floor duct trays and
cable trays in ceilings in addition to or in place of conventional conduit in the
floor and walls? ☐ ☐ ☐

Comments: _____

_____

2. Are convenience outlets provided for standard electrical equipment: floor
vacuums, scrubbers, polishers, clocks, computer terminals, and audiovisual equipment? ☐ ☐ ☐

Comments: _____

_____

	YES	NO	N/A

3. Are outlets away from walls and pillars, and are they flush-floor mounted and capped? Floor monuments are not recommended.   ☐ ☐ ☐

   Comments: _____

   _____

4. Instead of fixed floor outlets, has a raised floor system been considered in all areas that may need electrical or communications relocation over the life of the project?   ☐ ☐ ☐

   Comments: _____

   _____

5. Is additional empty conduit run to areas in the library that may require electrical power or communications equipment in the future?   ☐ ☐ ☐

   Comments: _____

   _____

6. Is there at minimum a 1-inch dedicated conduit with a home run from every data outlet to the telecommunications room? Another ¾-inch conduit is required for power.   ☐ ☐ ☐

   Comments: _____

   _____

7. Do automated systems have dedicated data lines?   ☐ ☐ ☐

   Comments: _____

   _____

8. Is the "sweep" on conduit runs gradual enough to accommodate fiber optic and coaxial cables?   ☐ ☐ ☐

   Comments: _____

   _____

9. Does every public seat in the library have access to a duplex receptacle for power and to data communications and/or telephone outlets? All outlets should provide duplex power receptacles, and space for at least four data ports (coaxial, fiber, and twisted pair wires, with a box large enough to accommodate all four types of wire).   ☐ ☐ ☐

   Comments: _____

   _____

10. Does every staff workstation have three to five duplex outlets and data communications/telephone outlets?   ☐ ☐ ☐

    Comments: _____

    _____

11. Are all cords and cables protected and out of sight?   ☐ ☐ ☐

    Comments: _____

    _____

12. Are dedicated lines provided for equipment requiring them?   ☐ ☐ ☐

    Comments: _____

    _____

	YES	NO	N/A

13. Before floors are poured or conduit is enclosed in walls, will the architect, contractor, and library staff "walk" the site to make sure that outlets are properly placed? ☐ ☐ ☐

    Comments: _____

    _____

14. Has a backup power source been considered for when the power is out? ☐ ☐ ☐

    Comments: _____

    _____

D. Lighting

1. Have the following lighting guidelines been followed?

   a) Maximize use of day lighting and integrate into electric lighting schemes. ☐ ☐ ☐

   b) Provide light-colored surfaces. Light-colored stack areas are critical. ☐ ☐ ☐

   c) Use task lighting at tables. ☐ ☐ ☐

   d) Use occupancy sensors for switching fixtures whenever possible. ☐ ☐ ☐

   e) Use dimming systems that are coupled to the amount of daylight within the space. ☐ ☐ ☐

   f) Increase the reflectance of walls (within contrast ratios). ☐ ☐ ☐

   g) Reduce glare by correctly choosing and placing fixtures. ☐ ☐ ☐

   h) Have a minimum number of different lamp types at the building and site. ☐ ☐ ☐

   i) Reduce the number of decorative and display lights. ☐ ☐ ☐

   j) Provide a combination of lighting types. Include both general diffuse (indirect) and direct lighting. ☐ ☐ ☐

   k) Avoid large brightness ratios. Because brightness is a function of reflectance and illumination, the brightness level is controllable through good design. ☐ ☐ ☐

   l) Provide fixture locations that allow easy lamp replacement. Staff should not have to move furniture and equipment and bring in a scaffold in order to re-lamp light fixtures. ☐ ☐ ☐

   Comments: _____

   _____

2. Is lighting energy- and cost-efficient? ☐ ☐ ☐

   Comments: _____

   _____

3. Will the building be designed to take advantage of natural light? Care must be taken to not cause glare or inconsistent light for users as well as to not damage books and furniture. ☐ ☐ ☐

   Comments: _____

   _____

	YES	NO	N/A

4. Have the advantages of natural light been considered?

   a) Enhanced visual quality ☐ ☐ ☐

   b) Connection to nature ☐ ☐ ☐

   c) Reduced energy cost ☐ ☐ ☐

   d) Reduced HVAC&R ☐ ☐ ☐

   e) Less use of energy resources ☐ ☐ ☐

   Comments: _____

5. If day lighting is used, can it be controlled by window coverings, tinted glass, or other special glazing? ☐ ☐ ☐

   Comments: _____

6. When natural lighting is used, is it designed to eliminate glare and "hot spots" of intense light and/or heat? ☐ ☐ ☐

   Comments: _____

7. Can all interior and exterior lights be controlled from one location? ☐ ☐ ☐

   Comments: _____

8. Can staff operate a light control at staff entrances, allowing adequate illumination before arriving at the main control point for interior lighting? ☐ ☐ ☐

   Comments: _____

9. Are light switches located where they can be easily and logically accessed, not behind door swings or large pieces of equipment? ☐ ☐ ☐

   Comments: _____

10. Is the building's night lighting adequate to allow observation of the library's interior through outside windows? ☐ ☐ ☐

    Comments: _____

11. Are rheostat (dimmer) controls available at individual workstations to permit local adjustment to user need? ☐ ☐ ☐

    Comments: _____

12. Are the following lighting levels maintained?

    a) *Reading areas:* 50 foot-candles average, measured horizontally at desktop and augmented with task lighting at carrels and tables where appropriate ☐ ☐ ☐

	YES	NO	N/A

b) *Stacks:* 20 foot-candles minimum sustained uniformly at floor level   ☐ ☐ ☐

c) *Conference or study rooms:* 30 to 40 foot-candles average measured horizontally at desktop   ☐ ☐ ☐

d) *Staff areas:* 50 foot-candles average on desks or worktables measured horizontally at desktop   ☐ ☐ ☐

e) *Large meeting or community rooms:* 40 foot-candles average with all lights on and with separately controlled lighting for the podium or front of the room   ☐ ☐ ☐

f) *Parking lot:* 0.6 foot-candles minimum measured horizontally on pavement to achieve a 4:1 average to minimum ratio, and with no spill light on adjacent properties. Lighting must be sensitive to neighbors, have a higher illumination level adjacent to the building and paths, and have a flexible control system that can be adjusted by staff.   ☐ ☐ ☐

Comments: _____

_____

13. Are ambient and task lights on timers or motion detectors in closed stacks, offices, and/or public areas?   ☐ ☐ ☐

Comments: _____

_____

14. Can ambient lighting be dimmed or brightened according to need?   ☐ ☐ ☐

Comments: _____

_____

15. Is lighting zoned so various areas can be dimmed or brightened independently?   ☐ ☐ ☐

Comments: _____

_____

16. Is flexible, timed programming available for each lighting zone?   ☐ ☐ ☐

Comments: _____

_____

17. Do switch labels identify light zones?   ☐ ☐ ☐

Comments: _____

_____

18. Can daylight be used as a source of lighting?   ☐ ☐ ☐

Comments: _____

_____

19. Are computer monitors and other video screens shielded from direct sunlight or glare? ☐ ☐ ☐

Comments: _____

_____

20. Can lighting be easily moved if furniture, shelving, or equipment is moved?   ☐ ☐ ☐

Comments: _____

_____

	YES	NO	N/A

21. Are components of the lighting system easily replaced and maintained? ☐ ☐ ☐

    Comments: _____

    _____

22. Are exterior lighting fixtures of vandal-resistant construction? ☐ ☐ ☐

    Comments: _____

    _____

23. Do exterior lighting fixtures have durable finishes to protect them from weather? ☐ ☐ ☐

    Comments: _____

    _____

24. Has the number of different lamp types been minimized to simplify maintenance and lamp stocking? ☐ ☐ ☐

    Comments: _____

    _____

25. Are replacement lamps

    a) Easily accessible? ☐ ☐ ☐

    b) Reasonably priced? ☐ ☐ ☐

    Comments: _____

    _____

26. Is there an emergency lighting system? ☐ ☐ ☐

    Comments: _____

    _____

E. Plumbing and Restrooms

1. Do all plumbing and restroom facilities meet the ADA guidelines described throughout chapter 6? ☐ ☐ ☐

    Comments: _____

    _____

2. Are restrooms constructed according to local building codes? ☐ ☐ ☐

    Comments: _____

    _____

3. Are restrooms and drinking fountains located near stairs, elevators, and other permanent installations? This is desirable because these areas will not move, keeping them all together in a core. ☐ ☐ ☐

    Comments: _____

    _____

4. Are restrooms built above the level of the sewer system? ☐ ☐ ☐

    Comments: _____

    _____

		YES	NO	N/A

5. Does the number of sinks, toilets, and urinals meet local codes? ☐ ☐ ☐

Comments: _____

_____

6. Does the design of the restrooms accommodate one-third more toilets for women than men? ☐ ☐ ☐

Comments: _____

_____

7. Are the toilets wall-hung to facilitate cleaning? ☐ ☐ ☐

Comments: _____

_____

8. Are the toilets low-flow to conserve water? ☐ ☐ ☐

Comments: _____

_____

9. Have waterless urinals been considered? ☐ ☐ ☐

Comments: _____

_____

10. Have the best quality fixtures and accessories been selected? The best quality fixtures should be selected because there usually is a limited budget, if any, for replacing equipment, and because of the heavy use the fixtures will receive. ☐ ☐ ☐

Comments: _____

_____

11. Are the restrooms

   a) Well ventilated (including fans)? ☐ ☐ ☐

   b) Well lit? ☐ ☐ ☐

   c) Soundproof? ☐ ☐ ☐

   d) Vandal-resistant, especially the wall and stall surfaces? ☐ ☐ ☐

Comments: _____

_____

12. Are there provisions for the following?

   a) Toilet paper ☐ ☐ ☐

   b) Soa ☐ ☐ ☐

   c) Trash receptacles ☐ ☐ ☐

   d) Towel dispensers or hand dryers ☐ ☐ ☐

   e) Sanitary napkin dispensers ☐ ☐ ☐

   f) Other _____ ☐ ☐ ☐

Comments: _____

_____

	YES	NO	N/A

13. Are dispensers planned and mounted to accommodate a change of vendors without damaging wall surfaces? ☐ ☐ ☐

   Comments: _____

   _____

14. Are there shelves for holding books and papers? ☐ ☐ ☐

   Comments: _____

   _____

15. Is there lockable closet/room storage for supplies? ☐ ☐ ☐

   Comments: _____

   _____

16. Are diaper-changing facilities available in all restrooms? ☐ ☐ ☐

   Comments: _____

   _____

F. Elevators and Escalators

1. Are elevators/escalators located away from quiet areas? ☐ ☐ ☐

   Comments: _____

   _____

2. Are there separate elevators for the public, staff, and/or freight? ☐ ☐ ☐

   Comments: _____

   _____

3. Do elevators/escalators meet ADA guidelines? ☐ ☐ ☐

   Comments: _____

   _____

4. Do elevators/escalators meet all local codes? ☐ ☐ ☐

   Comments: _____

   _____

5. Will the elevator/escalator system be designed so that routine maintenance will have minimal impact on library operations? ☐ ☐ ☐

   Comments: _____

   _____

11

Safety and Security

	YES	NO	N/A

A. General

1. Have all local codes regarding the safety of the occupants, building, and contents been met? ☐ ☐ ☐

   Comments: _____

   _____

2. Do the security measures provide a benefit of increased customer and staff safety without projecting a negative "police state" image? ☐ ☐ ☐

   Comments: _____

   _____

3. Do all alarm systems meet local codes when furnishings and decorations are in place? ☐ ☐ ☐

   Comments: _____

   _____

4. If the building is located in an earthquake zone, are all seismic protection measures in place? ☐ ☐ ☐

   Comments: _____

   _____

B. External Security

1. Does the building require fencing to control access to the property? ☐ ☐ ☐

   Comments: _____

   _____

	YES	NO	N/A
2. Is there sufficient, tamper-proof security lighting?	☐	☐	☐

Comments: _____

_____

	YES	NO	N/A
3. Can a person climbing trees, fences, the building structure, and so on gain access to roofs, upper windows, and ledges?	☐	☐	☐

Comments: _____

_____

	YES	NO	N/A
4. If HVAC&R and electrical systems are in sheds or buildings outside the main building, are security screens provided to keep people from entering?	☐	☐	☐

Comments: _____

_____

	YES	NO	N/A
5. Does the landscaping contribute to security by providing barriers to unauthorized entry?	☐	☐	☐

Comments: _____

_____

6. Are all vulnerable access points (doors, windows, air vents, etc.) protected against illegal entry with the following?

	YES	NO	N/A
a) High-security locks and hinges	☐	☐	☐
b) Security glazing	☐	☐	☐
c) Barriers (fences, grilles)	☐	☐	☐
d) Alarm systems	☐	☐	☐
e) Lighting systems	☐	☐	☐

Comments: _____

_____

7. Does the intrusion alarm

	YES	NO	N/A
a) Transmit to the police or a security company?	☐	☐	☐
b) Immediately notify library personnel?	☐	☐	☐
c) Have automatic reset?	☐	☐	☐
d) Have manual override?	☐	☐	☐

Comments: _____

_____

	YES	NO	N/A
8. Are exterior book drops theft- and tamper-proof?	☐	☐	☐

Comments: _____

_____

C. Internal Security

	YES	NO	N/A
1. Is there a materials theft-detection system with alarm?	☐	☐	☐

Comments: _____

_____

		YES	NO	N/A
2.	Does the alarm transmit to a control or circulation desk?	☐	☐	☐
	Comments: _____			
3.	Are windows and emergency exits wired to prevent illegal use?	☐	☐	☐
	Comments: _____			
4.	Is there an emergency lighting system?	☐	☐	☐
	Comments: _____			
5.	Are all emergency exits clearly marked with lighted signs?	☐	☐	☐
	Comments: _____			
6.	Are exhibits, rare-book collections, and other valuable materials provided with secure rooms and/or cases?	☐	☐	☐
	Comments: _____			
7.	Is valuable equipment attached to fixtures with security hardware?	☐	☐	☐
	Comments: _____			
8.	Can patrons gain undetected access to nonpublic areas?	☐	☐	☐
	Comments: _____			
9.	Are there secluded areas that require convex mirrors or closed-circuit TV?	☐	☐	☐
	Comments: _____			
10.	Are there areas where patrons can be undetected at closing?	☐	☐	☐
	Comments: _____			
11.	Is there an after-hours motion-detector system in place?	☐	☐	☐
	Comments: _____			
12.	If the building has a security staff, is their desk/office in a prominent location in order to act as a deterrent?	☐	☐	☐
	Comments: _____			

	YES	NO	N/A

D. Fire Safety

1. Is the building protected by a fire-detection system, including smoke detectors?   ☐ ☐ ☐

   Comments: _____

2. Are smoke detectors adequately distributed?   ☐ ☐ ☐

   Comments: _____

3. Does the alarm transmit to a fire station or central alarm station?   ☐ ☐ ☐

   Comments: _____

4. Are fire hoses and extinguishers adequately distributed and highly portable?   ☐ ☐ ☐

   Comments: _____

5. Is the building located close to a fire hydrant?   ☐ ☐ ☐

   Comments: _____

6. Is there a sprinkler system?   ☐ ☐ ☐

   Comments: _____

7. Is shelving equipped with top panels to protect contents from water damage?   ☐ ☐ ☐

   Comments: _____

8. Are there areas that require special fire suppression systems?
   a) Multiple-level, open stacks   ☐ ☐ ☐
   b) Rare-book collections   ☐ ☐ ☐
   c) Information labs and computer commons   ☐ ☐ ☐

   Comments: _____

E. Disaster Planning

The American Library Association website has a section providing a variety of resources to deal with disasters. It contains almost everything that a library needs to plan for or to handle a disaster: www.ala.org/ala/aboutala/offices/wo/woissues/disaster preparedness/distrprep.cfm.

1. Has the library prepared plans to manage natural and human-made disasters?   ☐ ☐ ☐
   - Natural disasters and hazards include floods, hurricanes, thunderstorms, tornadoes, extreme heat or cold, earthquakes, landslides, and fires.

	YES	NO	N/A

- Human-made threats include: shootings, biological threats, chemical threats, nuclear blasts, and radiation.

Comments: _____

_____

2. Does the plan have the following components?

   a) Introduction—stating the lines of authority and the possible events covered by the plan. ☐ ☐ ☐

   b) Actions to be taken if advance warning is available. ☐ ☐ ☐

   c) First-response procedures, including who should be contacted first in each type of emergency, what immediate steps should be taken, and how staff or teams will be notified. ☐ ☐ ☐

   d) Emergency procedures with sections devoted to each emergency event covered by the plan. This will include what is to be done during the event, and the appropriate salvage procedures to be followed once the first excitement is over. Floor plans should be included to illustrate what might be taking place in different parts of the library. ☐ ☐ ☐

   e) A rehabilitation plan for getting the library back to normal after the event. ☐ ☐ ☐

   f) Appendixes, which may include evacuation/floor plans; listing of emergency services; listing of emergency response team members and responsibilities; telephone tree; location of keys; fire/intrusion alarm procedures; listing of collection priorities; arrangements for relocation of the collections; listing of in-house supplies; listing of outside suppliers and services; insurance information; listing of volunteers; prevention checklist; record-keeping forms for objects moved in salvage efforts; detailed salvage procedures. ☐ ☐ ☐

   Comments: _____

   _____

3. Are the plans integrated into a larger campus or community plan? ☐ ☐ ☐

   Comments: _____

   _____

4. Does the library have building escape plans? ☐ ☐ ☐

   Comments: _____

   _____

5. If so, how will they be communicated to customers and staff? _____

   _____

   Comments: _____

   _____

6. Do staff members know how to shut off gas, electricity, and other utilities? ☐ ☐ ☐

   Comments: _____

   _____

7. Does the library have a first-aid kit? ☐ ☐ ☐

   Comments: _____

   _____

	YES	NO	N/A

8. Does the library have an area to accommodate a person who needs aid for medical or other reasons? This usually requires a cot or at least a recliner chair. ☐ ☐ ☐

   Comments: _____

   _____

9. Will the library be used as a shelter during a campus or community disaster? ☐ ☐ ☐

   Comments: _____

   _____

10. Does the library have a backup plan for critical documents and records? ☐ ☐ ☐

    Comments: _____

    _____

11. Does the library have a plan to mitigate damages to wet books and documents? ☐ ☐ ☐

    Comments: _____

    _____

12. Does the library have a plan to mitigate the damages from fire including reducing odor and cleaning soot-damaged materials? ☐ ☐ ☐

    Comments: _____

    _____

13. How will the library handle infrastructure outages including power outages, drops, or surges; utility outages; telecommunications failure; corrupt data; etc.? _____

    _____

    Comments: _____

    _____

14. Is a plan in place to deal with sabotage to library systems by customers or staff? ☐ ☐ ☐

    Comments: _____

    _____

12

Maintenance of Library Buildings and Property

	YES	NO	N/A

A. Routine Maintenance

1. Has a maintenance checklist been prepared for the custodial crew as well as for library staff who are responsible for checking that the work has been accomplished? ☐ ☐ ☐

   Comments: _____

   _____

2. Are maintenance supplies selected that will not emit air contaminants during use and storage? ☐ ☐ ☐

   Comments: _____

   _____

3. Are supplies stored in sealed, clearly labeled containers? ☐ ☐ ☐

   Comments: _____

   _____

4. Are chemicals, chemical-containing wastes, and containers disposed of according to manufacturers' instructions? ☐ ☐ ☐

   Comments: _____

   _____

5. Have dust-control procedures been established?

   a) Are there barrier mats at the entrances? ☐ ☐ ☐

   b) Are high-efficiency vacuum bags used? ☐ ☐ ☐

	YES	NO	N/A
c) Are feather dusters wrapped with a dust cloth?	☐	☐	☐
d) Are air return grilles and air supply vents cleaned?	☐	☐	☐

Comments: _____

_____

6. In cleaning floors,

	YES	NO	N/A
a) Has a schedule been established for vacuuming and mopping floors?	☐	☐	☐
b) Are spills on floors cleaned as soon as possible after they occur?	☐	☐	☐
c) Is restorative maintenance done as needed as well as on a general schedule? For example, heavily traveled carpets are cleaned twice a year, and carpeting is replaced every ten years.	☐	☐	☐

Comments: _____

_____

7. For plumbing fixtures and traps,

	YES	NO	N/A
a) Are drains checked for proper drainage at least once a week?	☐	☐	☐
b) Are floor drains checked for proper drainage at least once a week?	☐	☐	☐
c) Are toilets checked for proper flushing once a week?	☐	☐	☐

Comments: _____

_____

8. To control moisture, leaks, and spills,

	YES	NO	N/A
a) Is the building checked for moldy odors at least once a week?	☐	☐	☐
b) Are ceiling tiles, floors, and walls checked for leaks and discolorations at least once a week?	☐	☐	☐
c) Are bathrooms and sinks checked for leaks on a daily basis?	☐	☐	☐
d) Are windows, windowsills, and window frames free of condensate?	☐	☐	☐

Comments: _____

_____

9. Are appliances checked for odors and/or leaks? ☐ ☐ ☐

Comments: _____

_____

10. To control pests,

	YES	NO	N/A
a) Are the building and grounds checked for pest evidence, entry points, food, water, and harborage sites?	☐	☐	☐
b) Are all potential pest habitats in buildings and on the grounds inspected and monitored?	☐	☐	☐
c) Have alternative methods for treating pests been identified before pesticides are used?	☐	☐	☐

	YES	NO	N/A

d) Is a spot-treatment (or bait, crack, and crevice applications) used whenever pests are seen? This will reduce the amount of pesticide that will need to be used. ☐ ☐ ☐

e) Are records kept of pesticide use, and do the records meet all the local and state requirements? ☐ ☐ ☐

Comments: _____

_____

B. Graffiti

1. If graffiti occurs, is there a program in place to remove it as soon as possible? ☐ ☐ ☐

Comments: _____

_____

2. Does the landscaping create a barrier to help protect against vandalism? ☐ ☐ ☐

Comments: _____

_____

3. Is vegetation such as clinging vines used to cover walls to discourage graffiti? ☐ ☐ ☐

Comments: _____

_____

4. Are planter boxes used to protect walls? ☐ ☐ ☐

Comments: _____

_____

5. Will landscaping develop a dense mass against a wall so there is no room for graffiti? ☐ ☐ ☐

Comments: _____

_____

6. Is the building protected with a special coating or type of paint that allows for easy graffiti removal? ☐ ☐ ☐

Comments: _____

_____

7. Does the concrete used have a color or pigmentation to discourage graffiti? ☐ ☐ ☐

Comments: _____

_____

8. Is there security lighting to discourage graffiti? ☐ ☐ ☐

Comments: _____

_____

9. Are fixtures high enough on walls to protect them from vandalism? ☐ ☐ ☐

Comments: _____

_____

	YES	NO	N/A

10. Are fixtures sturdy enough to protect them from vandalism?   ☐ ☐ ☐
Comments: _____
_____

11. Are signs high enough off the ground to protect them from vandalism?   ☐ ☐ ☐
Comments: _____
_____

12. Is masonry or stone being used to protect areas that are particularly vulnerable to graffiti?   ☐ ☐ ☐
Comments: _____
_____

13. Is the entrance secure from theft, vandalism, and graffiti?   ☐ ☐ ☐
Comments: _____
_____

14. Is the building well lit, with light directed toward vulnerable areas and walkways?   ☐ ☐ ☐
Comments: _____
_____

C. Building Materials

1. Are exterior walls constructed of durable and easily maintained materials?   ☐ ☐ ☐
Comments: _____
_____

2. Are windows built to help protect against direct sunlight and glare?   ☐ ☐ ☐
Comments: _____
_____

3. Can locally abundant building materials be used in the construction?   ☐ ☐ ☐
Comments: _____
_____

4. Are the materials used energy efficient?   ☐ ☐ ☐
Comments: _____
_____

5. Is the building constructed of fire-resistant materials?   ☐ ☐ ☐
Comments: _____
_____

6. Are the materials used durable and of good quality?   ☐ ☐ ☐
Comments: _____
_____

	YES	NO	N/A

7. Have natural colors and finishes been used? ☐ ☐ ☐
   Comments: _____

   _____

8. Have colors that would quickly become outdated been avoided? ☐ ☐ ☐
   Comments: _____

   _____

9. Do the colors and finishes complement the character of the surrounding community? ☐ ☐ ☐
   Comments: _____

   _____

D. Custodial Facilities

1. Is there adequate locking storage space allocated for janitorial supplies, tools, maintenance equipment, etc., on each floor? ☐ ☐ ☐
   Comments: _____

   _____

2. Is a sink or running water available in the custodial room? ☐ ☐ ☐
   Is the floor sloped with a floor drain? ☐ ☐ ☐
   Comments: _____

   _____

3. Is the custodial room located as centrally as possible? ☐ ☐ ☐
   Comments: _____

   _____

4. Is there a custodial clothes closet or locker? ☐ ☐ ☐
   Comments: _____

   _____

5. If so, does the door have a louver or vent? ☐ ☐ ☐
   Comments: _____

   _____

6. Is there a mop, broom, and brush rack? ☐ ☐ ☐
   Comments: _____

   _____

7. Is there a desk or worktable and tool storage area for minor repairs? ☐ ☐ ☐
   Comments: _____

   _____

8. Is the door wide enough for ease of moving equipment in and out of the space? ☐ ☐ ☐
   Comments: _____

   _____

	YES	NO	N/A

9. Is the wall area around the sink of a durable material to prevent water damage? ☐ ☐ ☐

Comments: _____

_____

E. Groundskeeper Facilities

1. Is there provision for secure storage of lawn mowers, snowblowers, and other equipment? ☐ ☐ ☐

Comments: _____

_____

2. Is there provision for adequate outside faucets and electrical outlets? ☐ ☐ ☐

Comments: _____

_____

3. Are faucets, irrigation equipment, and electrical outlets vandal proof? ☐ ☐ ☐

Comments: _____

_____

F. Trash Enclosures

1. Is there adequate exterior space allocated for the storing of trash? ☐ ☐ ☐

Comments: _____

_____

2. Is the trash area easily accessible from the building and from the street for pickup? ☐ ☐ ☐

Comments: _____

_____

3. Is adequate space allowed for garbage truck maneuvering and/or turnaround? ☐ ☐ ☐

Comments: _____

_____

4. Is the garbage bin hidden/camouflaged from public view with shrubs or a decorative wall? ☐ ☐ ☐

Comments: _____

_____

5. Is the area secure from scavenging? ☐ ☐ ☐

Comments: _____

_____

YES   NO   N/A

G. Betterments and Improvements

1. Does the library have a policy for betterments and improvements? Betterments and improvements are minor capital improvement projects with a spending threshold set by the university/community, school district, etc. Betterments and improvements extend the life, increase the productivity, or significantly improve the safety (for example, asbestos removal) of the building as opposed to repairs and maintenance that either restore the asset to, or maintain it at, its normal or expected service life. ☐   ☐   ☐

   Comments: _____

   _____

2. In order to qualify as a betterment and improvement, do the benefits from the project need to extend for a stated number of years? ☐   ☐   ☐

   Comments: _____

   _____

3. Does the library have a procedure for requesting betterments and improvements? ☐   ☐   ☐

   Comments: _____

   _____

4. Does the parent institution or board have a policy in place for approving requests? ☐   ☐   ☐

   Comments: _____

   _____

5. Are projects to correct safety issues given first priority? ☐   ☐   ☐

   Comments: _____

   _____

6. Are there minor capital improvement projects that are ineligible? For example, some institutions prohibit projects dealing with maintenance or repairs. ☐   ☐   ☐

   Comments: _____

   _____

Building Occupancy and Post-occupancy Evaluation

	YES	NO	N/A

A. Building Acceptance

1. Have a library representative, the contractor, the architect, and other interested parties conducted a building inspection to develop a punch list? A punch list is developed during a walk through the building at the end of construction to determine what is not finished. A contractor may develop a preliminary punch list and the walk-through refines and usually increases the list of items to be completed. ☐ ☐ ☐

   Comments: _____

2. Is there one person who documents problems or suggestions during the punch list walk-through? ☐ ☐ ☐

3. After the punch list walk-through is completed, is there

   a) A list of what needs to be fixed? ☐ ☐ ☐

   b) A list of what is missing, or what needs to be ordered? ☐ ☐ ☐

   c) A procedure for communicating the information to all the staff? ☐ ☐ ☐

   d) A plan and procedure to clear items on the punch list? ☐ ☐ ☐

   Comments: _____

4. Has the building received a certificate of occupancy from the local building official? A certificate of occupancy is a document issued by a building official certifying that all or a designated portion of a building complies with the provisions of the building code and permitting occupancy for the building's designated use. It is issued when the completed work complies with the submitted plans and applicable laws, all paperwork is completed, all necessary approvals

	YES	NO	N/A

have been obtained from other appropriate governmental agencies, all fees owed
to the governmental building department are paid, and all relevant violations are
resolved. A library cannot legally occupy the space without a certificate of occupancy. ☐ ☐ ☐

Comments: _____

_____

5. If a certificate of occupancy has not yet been received, can the library obtain a
    temporary certificate to allow movement of equipment and books into the building? ☐ ☐ ☐

    Comments: _____

    _____

6. When the building is accepted by the owner (library), will the architect and contractor provide

    a) As-built drawings that document what was really built? Often during
       construction, what is built may vary from the original drawings and
       corrections are made in the "as built" drawings. It is vital that the library have
       these drawings for future work in the building.   ☐ ☐ ☐

    b) Shop drawings from the contractor to the architect documenting what was
       built? These drawings provide detail that is not in the original set of drawings
       from the architect. Shop drawings are drawings, diagrams, schedules, and
       other data specially prepared for the building project by the contractor or
       a subcontractor, manufacturer, supplier, or distributor to illustrate some
       portion of the work. The shop drawing normally shows more detail than
       the construction documents. It is drawn to explain the fabrication and/or
       installation of the items to the manufacturer's production crew or contractor's
       installation crews. The contractor is obligated by the contract documents to
       submit shop drawings, product data, and samples for certain parts of the work
       to the architect.   ☐ ☐ ☐

    Comments: _____

    _____

7. Has a keying and access system been decided?   ☐ ☐ ☐

    Comments: _____

    _____

8. Will the contractor provide a set of keys to the library after building acceptance?
    The library should have consulted with the architect and contractor early in
    construction to determine what keys will be required.   ☐ ☐ ☐

    Comments: _____

    _____

9. Has a room numbering system been decided?   ☐ ☐ ☐

    Comments: _____

    _____

	YES	NO	N/A

B. Getting Ready for Occupancy

1. Will there be any organizational changes in the new building, and if so, have they been explained to staff? ☐ ☐ ☐

   Comments: _____

   _____

2. Has the library's budget been adjusted to accommodate the new building (additional staff, utilities, etc.)? ☐ ☐ ☐

   Comments: _____

   _____

3. Will the library be required to change regulations as a result of the new building? ☐ ☐ ☐

   Comments: _____

   _____

4. Have VIP and staff tours been scheduled throughout the building process to get people involved and energized? ☐ ☐ ☐

   Comments: _____

   _____

5. Have virtual tours been scheduled for the staff so that they can envision where they will be working? ☐ ☐ ☐

   Comments: _____

   _____

6. To help staff "psychologically prepare" for the new working conditions,

   a) Have they been involved in the initial planning? ☐ ☐ ☐

   b) Have they reviewed plans and models in order to make suggestions? ☐ ☐ ☐

   c) Have they been given an opportunity to "personalize" their workstations and work areas? ☐ ☐ ☐

   d) Have they had the opportunity to tour the building under construction? ☐ ☐ ☐

   Comments: _____

   _____

7. Has the anticipated increased use of the facility been planned for? ☐ ☐ ☐

   Comments: _____

   _____

8. Has all the furniture and equipment been ordered so that it will arrive at the time it is needed? ☐ ☐ ☐

   Comments: _____

   _____

                                                                    YES   NO   N/A

C. Moving

1. Will the library employ a library-moving specialist, or will the library move with
    internal resources?   ☐   ☐   ☐
    Comments: _____
    _____

2. Can the move to the new space be scheduled during the time when demand for
    library services is at its lowest level?   ☐   ☐   ☐
    Comments: _____
    _____

3. Has the library allowed adequate time from the ending of services in the old
    building to establishment of services in the new building? Libraries often
    underestimate the time required, especially in larger building projects.   ☐   ☐   ☐
    Comments: _____
    _____

4. Will the library need to be closed in order to move to the new space?   ☐   ☐   ☐
    Comments: _____
    _____

5. If the library needs to close, how long can it remain open before it needs to be closed to move into the
    new space? _____
    _____
    Comments: _____
    _____

6. If the building project is an expansion, will the library be able to operate during
    construction of the addition? This sometimes is not determined until the
    contractor starts construction.   ☐   ☐   ☐
    Comments: _____
    _____

7. What approval from the university, college, school district, library board, or city council is required to approve the
    date of closing and the duration? _____
    _____
    Comments: _____
    _____

8. How will library customers be notified about the closing, and what new procedures will be required for interim ser-
    vice? _____
    _____
    Comments: _____
    _____

                                                                        YES   NO   N/A

9.   How much of the existing collection, stacks, furniture, and equipment will be moved to the new building? _____
     _____

     Comments: _____
     _____

10. Has the amount to be moved been calculated and measured so that it will fit into
     the new space? This includes books and media, furniture, and anything that will
     be part of the new building.   ☐   ☐   ☐
     Comments: _____
     _____

11. Will the items being moved be cleaned before the move?   ☐   ☐   ☐
     Comments: _____
     _____

12. Have timetables and schedules been made to plan all stages of the move?   ☐   ☐   ☐
     Comments: _____
     _____

D. Post-occupancy Evaluation

1.   Will a post-occupancy evaluation be conducted? This is the process of diagnosing
     the technical, functional, and behavioral aspects of a completed building in order
     to accumulate information for future programming and design activities.   ☐   ☐   ☐
     Comments: _____
     _____

2.   When will the post-occupancy evaluation be conducted? Usually it takes place one year from the date when the
     certificate of occupancy is issued. One year allows four seasons of use. _____

     Comments: _____
     _____

3.   Was the building completed on time?   ☐   ☐   ☐
     Comments: _____
     _____

4.   Was the building completed within budget?   ☐   ☐   ☐
     Comments: _____
     _____

5.   Did the building meet the library's building program?   ☐   ☐   ☐
     Comments: _____
     _____

                                                    YES   NO   N/A

6.   If not, what caused variance from the building program? _____
     _____

     Comments: _____
     _____

7.   Does the staff like the building?   ☐   ☐   ☐
     Comments: _____
     _____

8.   If not, what can be changed to solve the problem? _____
     _____

     Comments: _____
     _____

9.   Has the library had problems in maintaining the building?   ☐   ☐   ☐
     Comments: _____
     _____

10. If so, what can be done to mitigate maintenance problems? _____
     _____

     Comments: _____
     _____

11. Did the architect provide all the services specified in his or her contract?   ☐   ☐   ☐
     Comments: _____
     _____

12. Was the architect responsive to the needs of the client?   ☐   ☐   ☐
     Comments: _____
     _____

13. Did the architect adequately represent the client in negotiations with all
     concerned parties?   ☐   ☐   ☐
     Comments: _____
     _____

14. Did the contractor maintain a clean and safe job site?   ☐   ☐   ☐
     Comments: _____
     _____

15. Did the contractor identify problems in the drawings and/or specifications during
     the project?   ☐   ☐   ☐
     Comments: _____
     _____

	YES	NO	N/A

16. During the shakedown period (usually the one-year warranty period after the building is accepted by the owner), were errors and/or omissions in the new building brought to the attention of the architect and contractor?   ☐ ☐ ☐

Comments: _____

_____

17. Were all errors and/or omissions resolved to the owner's satisfaction during the shakedown period?   ☐ ☐ ☐

Comments: _____

_____

18. If errors and omissions occurred, was it possible to determine who was responsible?

    a) Owner   ☐ ☐ ☐

    b) Architect   ☐ ☐ ☐

    c) Contractor   ☐ ☐ ☐

    d) Undetermined or out of the control of any of the players   ☐ ☐ ☐

Comments: _____

_____

19. In final evaluation, was the building project

    a) Planned and designed to reinforce the library as a center of the campus or community?   ☐ ☐ ☐

    b) Designed to provide for comfort and health as well as safety and security of the campus or community?   ☐ ☐ ☐

    c) Designed to make effective use of all available resources?   ☐ ☐ ☐

    d) Designed to address changing library needs over time by permitting flexibility and adaptability?   ☐ ☐ ☐

Comments: _____

_____

Groundbreaking and Dedication Ceremonies

	YES	NO	N/A

A. Planning

1. Does the parent institution (university, city, etc.) have procedures and protocols in place that must be followed? ☐ ☐ ☐

    Comments: _____

2. Has planning begun at least three months before the scheduled event? ☐ ☐ ☐

    Comments: _____

3. Is timing of the event tied to one or a few people? For example, schedules of the provost, mayor, key donor, and so on may determine the date and time. ☐ ☐ ☐

    Comments: _____

4. Have the key participants been informed of and agreed to the date and time of the event? ☐ ☐ ☐

    Comments: _____

5. Are the date and time convenient for all the people who may be interested in the event? ☐ ☐ ☐

    Comments: _____

	YES	NO	N/A

6. Are there other events occurring on campus or in the community that may conflict with the event? For example, don't schedule the dedication ceremony for the new life sciences library at the University of Michigan on the date of the Michigan/Ohio State football game. ☐ ☐ ☐

Comments: _____

_____

7. Have invitations to the event been sent out in a timely manner? (Allow at least one month before the event.) ☐ ☐ ☐

Comments: _____

_____

8. Has one person been designated as the coordinator for the event? ☐ ☐ ☐

Comments: _____

_____

9. Has it been determined who will speak at the event? ☐ ☐ ☐

Comments: _____

_____

10. Do speakers know their time limits, and is there a way to keep them within the limits? ☐ ☐ ☐

Comments: _____

_____

11. Are devoted, talented people assigned to handle the various jobs required to make the event successful? ☐ ☐ ☐

Comments: _____

_____

12. Do all the people working on the event know their roles and responsibilities? ☐ ☐ ☐

Comments: _____

_____

13. Has publicity been prepared and scheduled? ☐ ☐ ☐

Comments: _____

_____

14. Have press releases and informational packets been sent to the local media? ☐ ☐ ☐

Comments: _____

_____

15. Have the media been contacted and urged to cover the event? ☐ ☐ ☐

Comments: _____

_____

16. Has a media contact person been identified and listed in all publicity along with an address and telephone number? ☐ ☐ ☐

Comments: _____

_____

	YES	NO	N/A

17. Is someone responsible for making an audio and video history of the event? ☐ ☐ ☐
    Comments: _____
    _____

18. Is someone responsible for gathering and keeping memorabilia from the event such as a guest book, gifts, and the like? ☐ ☐ ☐
    Comments: _____
    _____

19. Will the event be short, interesting, and focused? ☐ ☐ ☐
    Comments: _____
    _____

B. Event Checklist

1. Have street closures, parking, and traffic control been coordinated with the local law authorities? ☐ ☐ ☐
   Comments: _____
   _____

2. Will the site be inspected and cleaned up before the event? ☐ ☐ ☐
   Comments: _____
   _____

3. Will there be adequate signage indicating where attendees are to go? ☐ ☐ ☐
   Comments: _____
   _____

4. For groundbreakings, will "ceremonial shovels" and hard hats be available? ☐ ☐ ☐
   Comments: _____
   _____

5. For dedications, will "ceremonial scissors" be available? ☐ ☐ ☐
   Comments: _____
   _____

6. Has a source been found to provide the following?
   a) Tables ☐ ☐ ☐
   b) Chairs ☐ ☐ ☐
   c) Podium ☐ ☐ ☐
   d) Barricades ☐ ☐ ☐
   e) Public-address system ☐ ☐ ☐
   f) Stage ☐ ☐ ☐
   g) Flags ☐ ☐ ☐
   h) Institutional seals ☐ ☐ ☐

	YES	NO	N/A
i) Refreshments	☐	☐	☐
j) Tablecloths, napkins, plates, silverware, and cups	☐	☐	☐
k) Trash cans/bags	☐	☐	☐
l) Plants or decorations	☐	☐	☐
m) Bathrooms and toilet supplies	☐	☐	☐

Comments: _____

_____

7. Have invitations been sent to the following?

	YES	NO	N/A
a) University or college administration	☐	☐	☐
b) Mayor	☐	☐	☐
c) City council	☐	☐	☐
d) Architect	☐	☐	☐
e) Contractor	☐	☐	☐
f) Project manager	☐	☐	☐
g) Friends of the Library	☐	☐	☐
h) Community groups	☐	☐	☐
i) Library VIPs	☐	☐	☐

Comments: _____

_____

8. Will name tags be available?   ☐ ☐ ☐

Comments: _____

_____

9. Will souvenirs or commemorative items be given to attendees?   ☐ ☐ ☐

Comments: _____

_____

10. Will VIPs receive special items?   ☐ ☐ ☐

Comments: _____

_____

11. Will a guest book be available, allowing event attendees to sign in?   ☐ ☐ ☐

Comments: _____

_____

12. Have invitations been

	YES	NO	N/A
a) Designed?	☐	☐	☐
b) Printed?	☐	☐	☐
c) Checked and checked again for accuracy?	☐	☐	☐
d) Mailed at least one month before the event?	☐	☐	☐
e) Saved for the library's archives?	☐	☐	☐

	YES	NO	N/A

Comments: _____

_____

13. Has the program been

    a) Designed?   ☐ ☐ ☐

    b) Printed?   ☐ ☐ ☐

    c) Checked and checked again for accuracy?   ☐ ☐ ☐

    d) Saved for the library's archives?   ☐ ☐ ☐

Comments: _____

_____

14. Is there a master of ceremonies for the event?   ☐ ☐ ☐

Comments: _____

_____

15. If so, how is that person selected? _____

Comments: _____

_____

16. Will speakers

    a) Know and adhere to their time limit?   ☐ ☐ ☐

    b) Provide the master of ceremonies with biographical information for introductions?   ☐ ☐ ☐

    c) Provide copies of their remarks for the library's archives?   ☐ ☐ ☐

    d) Know when to arrive and where to sit?   ☐ ☐ ☐

    e) Know the proper attire?   ☐ ☐ ☐

Comments: _____

_____

17. Will individuals be recognized for their contributions to the building project? This might include the architect, contractor, and so on.   ☐ ☐ ☐

Comments: _____

_____

18. Has music been arranged for the event?   ☐ ☐ ☐

Comments: _____

_____

19. Will there be a color guard for a national anthem/color ceremony?   ☐ ☐ ☐

Comments: _____

_____

20. If bad weather has the potential to affect the event, is an alternative plan in place?   ☐ ☐ ☐

Comments: _____

_____

	YES	NO	N/A
21. Will thank-you letters be sent to the following?			
a) Dignitaries	☐	☐	☐
b) Speakers	☐	☐	☐
c) Donors	☐	☐	☐
d) Volunteers	☐	☐	☐
e) Friends	☐	☐	☐
f) Staff	☐	☐	☐
g) Architects and construction crew	☐	☐	☐
h) Others _____	☐	☐	☐

Comments: _____

_____

	YES	NO	N/A
22. Will the site be cleaned after the event?	☐	☐	☐

Comments: _____

_____

Bibliography

Aaronson, Lauren. "An iPod for Your Books." *Popular Science,* August 2007, p. 17.

"ADA Standards for Accessible Design." U.S. Department of Justice (2007), 493–580, www.ada.gov/stdspdf.htm.

Allen, Walter C. "Selected References." *Library Trends* 36, no. 2 (1987): 475–91.

Bahr, Alice Harrison. "Library Buildings in a Digital Age: Why Bother?" *College and Research Libraries News* 61, no. 7 (2000): 590–91, 608.

Baumann, Charles H. *The Influence of Angus Snead Macdonald and the Snead Bookstack on Library Architecture.* Metuchen, NJ: Scarecrow Press, 1972.

Bazillion, Richard J., and Connie Braun. *Academic Libraries as High-Tech Gateways.* Chicago: American Library Association, 1995.

Bell, Steven J. "Design Thinking." *American Libraries* 39, no. 1 and 2 (2008): 44–49.

Bernheim, Anthony, AIA. "San Francisco Main Library: A Healthy Building." Paper presented at the IFLA Council and Conference, Barcelona, Spain, August 25, 1993.

Bisbrouck, Marie-Francoise, Jérémie Desjardins, Céline Ménil, Florence Poncé, François Rouyer-Gayette, eds. "Libraries as Places: Buildings for the 21st Century." Paper presented at the International Federation of Library Associations and Institutions, Paris, France, 2003.

Black, J. B., Janet Black, Ruth O'Donnell, and Jane Scheuerle. *Surveying Public Libraries for the ADA.* Tallahassee: Bureau of Library Development, Division of Library and Information Services, State Library of Florida, 1993.

Block, David. "Remote Storage in Research Libraries: A Microhistory." *Library Resources and Technical Services* 44, no. 4 (2000): 184–89.

Boaz, Martha. *A Living Library: Planning Public Library Buildings for Cities of 100,000 or Less.* Los Angeles: University of Southern California Press, 1957.

Boss, Richard W. *The Library Manager's Guide to Automation,* 2nd ed. White Plains: Knowledge Industry Publications, 1984.

———. *Telecommunications for Library Management.* White Plains: Knowledge Industry Publications, 1985.

———. *Information Technologies and Space Planning for Libraries and Information Centers.* Boston: G. K. Hall, 1987.

———. "Automated Storage/Retrieval and Return/Sorting Systems." Public Library Association, www.ala.org/ala/mgrps/divs/pla/plapublications/platechnotes/index.cfm.

Brawner, Lee, and Donald K. Beck Jr. *Determining Your Public Library's Future Size.* Chicago: American Library Association, 1996.

Breeding, Marshall. *Library LANs: Case Studies in Practice and Application.* Westport, CT: Meckler, 1992.

Brown, Carol R. *Selecting Library Furniture: A Guide for Librarians, Designers, and Architects.* Phoenix: Oryx Press, 1989.

Bryan, Cheryl, for the Public Library Association. *Managing Facilities for Results: Optimizing Space for Services.* Chicago: American Library Association, 2007.

California Library Association. *Earthquake Preparedness Manual for California Libraries.* Sacramento: California Library Association, 1990.

Campbell, Anne L. "Magical Models." *Library Journal* 128, no. 3 (2003): 38–40.

Carlson, Scott. "As Students Work Online, Reading Rooms Empty Out—Leading Some Campuses to Add Starbucks." *Chronicle of Higher Education* 48, no. 12 (2001): A35–A38.

———. "An Anthropologist in the Library." *Chronicle of Higher Education,* Information Technology Section 53, no. 50 (2007): 26.

Carroll, R. E. "Building a Library: The Librarian/Architect Relationship." *New Zealand Libraries* 45 (1987): 85–89.

Carvajal, Doreen. "Racing to Convert Books to Bytes." *New York Times* online, December 9, 1999, 7.

Cheek, Lawrence. "On Architecture: How the New Central Library Really Stacks Up." *Seattle Post-Intelligencer* (2007), http://seattlepi.nwsource.com/visualart/309029 _architecture27.html.

Ching, Francis D. K. *A Visual Dictionary of Architecture.* New York: Van Nostrand Reinhold, 1995.

Church, Jennifer. "The Evolving Information Commons." *Library Hi Tech* 23, no. 1 (2005).

Cohen, Elaine. "Library Facilities." *Bookmark* (Spring 1990): 210–12.

Cohen, Elaine, and Aaron Cohen. *Designing and Space Planning for Libraries: A Behavioral Guide.* New York: Bowker, 1979.

College and Research Libraries Task Force. "Standards for Libraries in Higher Education: A Draft." *College and Research Libraries News* 64, no. 5 (2003): 329–36.

Corban, Gaylan. E-mail, January 13, 1997.

Dahlgren, Anders C. "An Alternative to Library Building Standards." *Illinois Libraries* 67 (November 1985).

———. *Public Library Space Needs: A Planning Outline.* Madison: Wisconsin Department of Public Instruction, 1988.

———. *Planning Library Buildings: A Select Bibliography.* Chicago: Library Administration and Management Association, 1990.

Depew, John N. *A Library, Media, and Archival Preservation Handbook.* Santa Barbara: ABC-CLIO, 1991.

Dewe, Michael. *Library Buildings: Preparation for Planning Proceedings of the Seminar Held in Aberystwyth, August 10–14, 1987,* IFLA Publications 48. Munich, Germany: K. G. Saur, 1989.

Dreyfuss, Joel. "Bionic Books." *Modern Maturity* 43W, no. 5 (2000): 90, 92.

Dublin, Fred. "Mechanical Systems in Libraries." *Library Trends* 36 (Fall 1987): 351–60.

Eckelman, Carl A., and Yusuf Z. Erdil. "Test Reports on 15 Models of Bracket-Type Steel Library Bookstacks." *Library Technology Reports* 34, no. 6 (1998): 685–786.

Erikson, Rolf, and Carolyn Markuson. *Designing a School Library Media Center for the Future,* 2nd ed. Chicago: American Library Association, 2007.

Farmanfarmaian, Roxane. "Beyond E-Books: Glimpses of the Future." *Publishers Weekly* 248, no. 1 (2001): 56–57.

Fisher, Lawrence M. "Alliance to Send Video-on-Demand on the Web." *New York Times,* August 14, 2000, 3.

Fraley, Ruth A., and Carol Lee Anderson. *Library Space Planning: How to Assess, Allocate, and Reorganize Collections, Resources, and Physical Facilities.* New York: Neal-Schuman, 1990.

Gaines, Ervin, Marian Huttner, and Frances Peters. "Library Architecture: The Cleveland Experience." *Wilson Library Bulletin* 56, no. 8 (1982): 590–95.

Garbarine, Rachelle. "Residential Real Estate: A Computer Program for Apartment Managers." *New York Times,* August 18, 2000, 3.

Garcia, June, and Sandra Nelson for the Public Library Association. *Public Library Service Responses, 2007.* Chicago: American Library Association, 2007.

Garney, Beth A., and Ronald R. Powell. "Electronic Mail Reference Services in the Public Library." *Reference and User Services Quarterly* 39, no. 3 (2000): 249–52.

Graff, Susan. "Six Steps to Sustainability." *CRO: Corporate Responsibility Officer,* September 6, 2007.

Grant, Dorothy L., Thomas M. Grant, and Daniel S. Grant. *ADA Compliance Guidelines: California Access Code; Americans with Disabilities Act Title III—California Access Code Title 24.* San Diego: ACR Group, 1994.

Green, Joshua. "No Lectures or Teachers, Just Software." *New York Times*, August 10, 2000, 5.

Green, William R. *The Retail Store: Design and Construction.* New York: Van Nostrand Reinhold, 1991.

Guernsey, Lisa. "Bookbag of the Future." *New York Times* online, March 2, 2000, 7.

———. "The Library as the Latest Web Venture." *New York Times* online, June 15, 2000, 7.

———. "Scan the Headlines? No, Just the Bar Codes." *New York Times* online, May 4, 2000, 6.

Habich, Elizabeth Chamberlain. *Moving Library Collections: A Management Handbook.* Edited by Series Adviser Gerard B. McCabe, The Greenwood Library Management Collection. Westport, CT: Greenwood Press, 1998.

Hagiu, Andrei, and Bruno Jullien. "Designing a Two-Sided Platform: When to Increase Search Costs?" *Harvard Business School Working Knowledge for Business Leaders* (2007).

Hagloch, Susan B. *Library Building Projects: Tips for Survival.* Englewood, CO: Libraries Unlimited, 1994.

Hart, Thomas L. *The School Library Media Facilities Planner.* New York: Neal-Schuman, 2006.

Hawkins, Brian L., and Patricia Battin, eds. *The Mirage of Continuity: Reconfiguring Academic Information Resources for the 21st Century.* Washington, DC: Council on Library and Information Resources and Association of American Universities, 1998.

Henry, Karen H. *ADA: 10 Steps to Compliance.* Sacramento: California Chamber of Commerce, 1992.

Himmel, Ethel, and William James Wilson for the Public Library Association. *Planning for Results: A Public Library Transformation Process.* Chicago: American Library Association, 1998.

Holt, Raymond M. "Trends in Public Library Buildings." *Library Trends* 36 (Fall 1987): 267–85.

———. *Planning Library Buildings and Facilities: From Concept to Completion.* Metuchen, NJ: Scarecrow Press, 1989.

Holt, Raymond M., and Anders C. Dalhgren. *The Wisconsin Library Building Project Handbook,* 2nd ed. Madison: Wisconsin Department of Public Instruction, 1989.

Howe, Neil, and William Strauss. "The Next 20 Years: How Customer and Workforce Attitudes Will Evolve." *Harvard Business Review* 85, no. 7–8 (2007): 41–52.

Jones, Patrick. *Connecting Young Adults and Libraries: A How-to-Do-It Manual.* New York: Neal-Schuman, 1992.

Kirkpatrick, David D. "Random House Plans to Establish Exclusively Digital Unit." *New York Times*, July 31, 2000, 5.

Kirwin, William J. "What to Do until the Architect Comes." *North Carolina Libraries* 39 (Fall 1981): 5–8.

Klasing, Jane P. *Designing and Renovating School Library Media Centers.* Chicago: American Library Association, 1991.

Kolb, Audrey. *A Manual for Small Libraries.* Juneau: Alaska State Library, 1992.

Koontz, Christie. "Retail Interior Layout for Libraries." *Marketing Library Services* 19, no. 1 (2005): 1–4 (Electronic Articles).

Koontz, Christie, and Dean Jue. "Unlock Your Demographics." *Library Journal* 129, no. 4 (2004): 32–33.

Kroller, Franz. "Standards for Library Building." *Inspel* 16, no. 1 (1982): 40–44.

LaBrec, Raymond. "Playing 20 Questions." *San Diego Daily Transcript,* November 16, 1999, 9A.

Langmead, Stephen. *New Library Design: Guidelines to Planning Academic Library Buildings.* Toronto: John Wiley and Sons Canada, 1970.

Lehmann-Haupt, Christopher. "Creating 'the Last Book' to Hold All the Others." *New York Times*, April 8, 1998, 3.

Leibovich, Lori. "Choosing Quick Hits over the Card Catalog." *New York Times*, August 10, 2000, 6.

Levin-Epstein, Michael. "Pay Attention to Details." *Behavioral Healthcare,* April 1, 2007, 2.

Lewis, Christopher. "The Americans with Disabilities Act and Its Effect on Public Libraries." *Public Libraries* (January/February 1992): 23–28.

Lewis, Michael. "Boom Box." *New York Times Magazine,* August 18, 2000.

Lewis, Myron E., and Mark L. Nelson. "How to Work with an Architect." *Wilson Library Bulletin* 57 (September 1982): 44–46.

Library Administration and Management Association. *Building Blocks for Planning Functional Library Space.* Lanham, MD: Scarecrow Press, 2001.

———. *Library Buildings, Equipment and the ADA: Compliance Issues and Solutions.* Edited by Susan E. Cirillo and Robert E. Danford. Chicago: American Library Association, 1996.

Library of Michigan. *LSCA Builds Michigan Libraries.* Lansing: Library of Michigan, 1986.

Lushington, Nolan. "Getting It Right: Evaluating Plans in the Library Building Planning Process." *Library Administration and Management* 7, no. 3 (1993): 159–63.

Lushington, Nolan, and Willis N. Mills. *Libraries Designed for Users: A Planning Handbook.* Syracuse: Gaylord Professional Publications, 1979.

MacWhinnie, Laurie A. "The Information Commons: The Academic Library of the Future." *portal: Libraries and the Academy* 3, no. 2 (2003).

Maltby, Emily. "An ATM for Books: Coming Soon—The Most Inclusive Reader's Catalog in the World, at Your Fingertips." *Fortune Small Business Magazine; CNN Money.com* (2006), http://money.cnn.com/magazines/fsb/fsb_archive/2006/12/01/8395114/index.htm.

Markoff, John. "I.B.M. Device Raises Storage of Tiny PC's." *New York Times*, June 20, 2000, 3.

Martin, Ron G. "Libraries for the Future: Planning Buildings That Work." *Proceedings of the Library Buildings Preconference, June 27–28, 1991, Atlanta, Georgia.* Chicago: American Library Association, 1992.

Massmann, Ann. "The Wood Shelving Dilemma." *Library Resources and Technical Services* 44, no. 4 (2000): 209–14.

McCabe, Gerard B. *Operations Handbook for the Small Academic Library.* New York: Greenwood Press, 1989.

McCarthy, Richard C., AIA. *Designing Better Libraries: Selecting and Working with Building Professionals.* The Highsmith Press Handbook Series. Fort Atkinson, WI: Highsmith Press, 1995.

Mendels, Pamela. "Universities Adopt Computer Literacy Requirements." *New York Times* online, September 29, 1999, 3.

Merrill-Oldham, Jan, and Jutta Reed-Scott. "Library Storage Facilities, Management and Services." In *Systems and Procedures Exchange Center,* compiled by Jan Merrill-Oldham and Jutta Reed-Scott, 2. Washington, DC: Association of Research Libraries, Office of Leadership and Management Services, 1999.

Mervis, Sybil Stern. "How to Plan a Groundbreaking Ceremony for the Library." *Illinois Libraries* 77, no. 3 (1995): 123–27.

Metcalf, Keyes D. "Selection of Library Sites." *College and Research Libraries* 22 (May 1961): 183–92.

———. *Planning Academic and Research Library Buildings.* New York: McGraw-Hill, 1965.

Metcalf, Keyes D., Philip D. Leighton, and David C. Weber. *Planning Academic and Research Library Buildings,* 2nd ed. Chicago: American Library Association, 1986.

Michaels, Andrea. "Design Today." *Wilson Library Bulletin* 62, no. 8 (1988): 55–57.

Michigan State University Libraries, Center for Great Lakes Culture, and California Preservation Program. "Disaster Mitigation Planning Assistance Website." http://matrix.msu.edu/~disaster/index.php.

Miller, Kathy. "3M Unveils a Major New Library Technology System." *Computers in Libraries* (January 2000): 26–28.

Moore, Nick. *Measuring the Performance of Public Libraries.* Paris: UNESCO, 1989.

Mount, Ellis. *Creative Planning of Special Library Facilities.* New York: Haworth, 1988.

Natale, Joe. "Full and Equal Access: Americans with Disabilities Act." *Illinois Libraries* 73, no. 7 (1991): 599–602.

———. "The Next Step: The ADA Self-Evaluation." *Illinois Libraries* 73, no. 7 (1992): 599–602.

National Institute of Building Sciences (NIBS). "Whole Building Design Guide." The Institute, 2006.

Nelson, Sandra. *The New Planning for Results: A Streamlined Approach.* Chicago: American Library Association, 2001.

Novak, Gloria. "Movable Compact Shelving Systems: Selection and Specifications." *Library Technology Reports* 35, no. 5 (1999): 557–708.

O'Keefe, Brian. "The Smartest (or the Nuttiest) Futurist on Earth." *Fortune,* May 14, 2007, 60–69.

Oxner, Sheldon R. *How to Select a Contractor.* Omaha: Simmons-Boardman, 1979.

Pack, Todd. "E-Books Take Texts Down a Digital Track." *Orlando Sentinel,* July 15, 2000, 3.

Page, Kathryn. "Lighting Program for Libraries." Paper presented at the American Library Association Annual Conference, Chicago, 1995.

Patkus, Beth Lindblom, and Karen Motylewski. "Disaster Planning for Cultural Institutions." Nashville, TN: American Association for State and Local History, 1993.

Pine, B. Joseph, and James H. Gilmore. *The Experience Economy: Work Is Theatre and Every Business a Stage.* Boston: Harvard Business School Press, 1999.

Pollet, D. "New Directions in Library Signage: You Can Get There from Here." *Wilson Library Bulletin* 50 (1976): 456–62.

Popovec, Jennifer. "New Software Makes Green Building Easier." *National Real Estate Investor,* September 18, 2006.

"Project Management Academy: The Executive Challenge." San Diego, CA: City of San Diego, 1994.

Public Library Association. *Interim Standards for Small Public Libraries: Guidelines toward Achieving the Goals of Public Library Service.* Chicago: Public Library Association, 1962.

Richtel, Matt. "Trying to Close Technology Divide as Satellite Operators Battle Cable." *New York Times* online, April 15, 2003. www.nytimes.com/2003/04/15/business/media/15BIRD.html.

Rizzo, Joseph P., AIA. "Get with the Program! Building a Vision of Place." *Library Journal* 127 (December 15, 2002): 66–68.

Roberts, Regina Lee. "The Evolving Landscape of the Learning Commons." *Library Review* 56, no. 9 (2007).

Rohlf, Robert H. "The Selection of an Architect." *Public Libraries* 21 (Spring 1982): 5–8.

———. "New Factor in Planning Public Library Buildings." *Public Libraries* 26 (Summer 1987): 52–53.

———. "Best-Laid Plans: A Consultant's Constructive Advice." *School Library Journal* 36 (February 1990): 28–31.

Rohlf, Robert H., and David R. Smith. "Public Library Site Selection." *Public Libraries* 24 (Summer 1985): 47–49.

Rush, Richard D. "The Library of the Future." *Construction Specifier* (October 1999): 41–44, 58.

Sager, Don, ed. "Changing Perspectives: Joint Use of Facilities by Schools and Public Libraries." *Public Libraries* 38, no. 6 (1999): 355–59.

Sands, Johanna. "Sustainable Library Design." Sacramento: California State Library, 2002.

Sannwald, William W. *Checklist of Library Building Design Considerations,* 4th ed. Chicago: American Library Association, 2001.

———. *Mira Mesa Branch Library Building Program.* San Diego: San Diego Public Library, 1990.

———. *Event Checklist for Library Groundbreakings and Openings.* San Diego: San Diego Public Library, 1993.

———. "Inspiring Library Spaces from the USA." *Public Library Journal* 21, no. 5 (2006): 3–7.

Schibsted, Evantheia. "The Fine Art of Choosing an Architect." *Edutopia* (July/August 2007): 30–32.

Schibsted, Evantheia, and J. J. Sulin. "Going Green: In Chicago's Urban Sprawl, an Environmentally Friendly School Blooms." *Edutopia* 1, no. 9 (2006): 24–28.

Schott, Virginia O. "Site Selection for Rural Public Libraries." *Rural Libraries* 7, no. 2 (1987): 27–59.

Seal, Robert A. "The Information Commons Handbook." *portal: Libraries and the Academy* 7, no. 3 (2007).

Shelton, John A. *Seismic Safety Standards for Library Shelving, California State Library Manual of Recommended Practice.* Sacramento: California State Library Association, 1990.

Showley, Roger. "Sony's Metreon Is the Disneyland of the New Millennium." *San Diego Union Tribune,* September 5, 1999, 6.

Silberman, Steve. "Ex Libris: The Joys of Curling Up with a Good Digital Reading Device." *Wired,* July 1998, 98–104.

Silver, Cy H. "Construction Standards for California Public Libraries." *Library Administration and Management* 4, no. 2 (1990): 82–86.

Simon, Matthew J., and George Yourke. "Building a Solid Architect-Client Relationship." *Library Administration and Management* 1 (June 1987): 100–104.

Singh, Rajwant. "Standards and Specifications for Library Buildings." *Lucknow Librarian* 15, no. 2 (1983): 65–73.

Smith, David Conda. "Communication Design: The Use of Visual Cues in the Environment to Aid in Wayfinding with Contextual Essay." Union Institute and University, 2007.

Smith, Fran Kellogg, and Fred J. Bertolone. *Bringing Interiors to Light.* New York: Watson-Guptill, 1986.

Smith, Lester K. *Planning Library Buildings: From Decision to Design.* Chicago: American Library Association, 1986.

Spencer, Mary Ellen. "Evolving a New Model: The Information Commons." *Reference Services Review* 34, no. 2 (2006).

Strauch, Katina. "Selling Points: Shops in the Library." *Wilson Library Bulletin* 68 (February 1994): 45–47.

Teachout, Terry. "A Hundred Books in Your Pocket: The E-Book Will Transform Reading—and Writing." *Wall Street Journal,* January 21, 2006, 14.

U.S. Environmental Protection Agency. "IAQ Tools for Schools Kit: Building and Grounds Maintenance Checklist," www.epa.gov/iedweb00/schools/toolkit.html.

U.S. Green Building Council. "An Introduction to the U.S. Green Building Council and the LEED™ Green Building Rating System." U.S. Green Building Council, www.usgbc.org.

Veatch, Lamar. "Toward the Environmental Design of Library Buildings." *Library Trends* 36 (February 1987): 45–47.

Weber, Thomas E. "Will Web Publishers Reshape Book Industry or Just Flood Market?" *Wall Street Journal,* July 3, 2000, B1.

Weiss, Jonathan C., Kath Williams, and Judith Heerwagen. "How to Design for Humans." *Architecture,* April 1, 2004, 2.

Wheeler, Joseph, and Alfred Morton. *The American Public Library: Its Planning and Design with Special Reference to Its Administration and Service.* Chicago: American Library Association, 1941.

Wilgoren, Jodi. "A Revolution in Education Clicks into Place." *New York Times,* March 26, 2000, 4.

Winters, Willis C., and Brad Waters. "On the Verge of a Revolution: Current Trends in Library Lighting." *Library Trends* 36 (Fall 1987): 327–59.

Wolf, Gary. "Exploring the Unmaterial World." *Wired* 8, no. 6 (June 2000): 308–19.

Wood, Lamont. "Copper for Fiber: Fiber Optics into the Home, with Help from DSL." *Scientific American* 293, no. 1 (2005): 24.

Yegyazarian, Anush. "Tech.Gov: World Wide Library?" *PC World: Technology Perspective Newsletter* (2005).

You may also be interested in

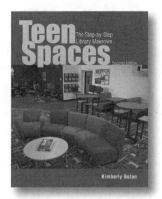

Teen Spaces, 2nd ed.: Revising the first practical guide to creating inviting spaces for teens in the library, Bolan reveals what it takes for your makeover to go as smoothly as possible. You'll find step-by-step instructions and easy-to-use templates; updated tools, worksheets, instructions, and vendor information; inspiring illustrations and discussions of what other libraries have achieved; and much more.

Designing a School Library Media Center for the Future, 2nd ed.:
Designing a school library media center may be a once-in-a-lifetime opportunity, so take advantage! In this hands-on guidebook, school library construction and media specialists Rolf Erikson and Carolyn Markuson share their experiences of working on more than 100 media center building projects around the country, using conceptual plans from actual school libraries. With thirty new illustrations and floor plans and an updated glossary of technical terms, readers will be knowledgeable and organized when discussing plans with contractors and vendors. Using the guidance here, you'll avoid the classic building and renovation hazards and build a library media center for the future!

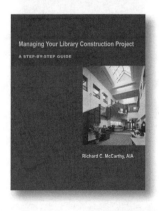

Managing Your Library Construction Project: Richard McCarthy is an 18-year veteran library trustee and architect with in-depth expertise building libraries. In this resource he communicates the challenges and opportunities faced when building and designing a library from both sides of the table. This authoritative overview is filled with practical advice for understanding key relationships and managing a complex process. Library directors, professionals, administrators, and trustees will get well-informed answers to their questions.

Managing Facilities for Results: Carving out new service areas within existing space, forgoing massive additions or expensive new buildings, offers a cost-effective solution for budget-conscious libraries. With examples ranging from small to large public libraries, the process outlined here is equally valuable for school, special, and academic librarians who are faced with space repurposing challenges. This guide will help you create a blueprint that prioritizes services and creates the space for them within your existing facility.

For more information, please visit www.alastore.ala.org.